JN069599

The Minimal English Test

牧 秀樹
何 海希

大学入学共通テスト 読解版

最小英語テスト（MET） ドリル

大学入学
共通テスト
読解版

開拓社

まえがき

　「大学入学共通テスト英語の読解問題に**慣れておきたい。**」そんな方に，このドリルをお勧めします。『**最小英語テスト（MET）ドリル**』の**第7弾**です。高校生，大学生，社会人，そして，英語からしばらく遠ざかっている方にも楽しんでいただけます。

　音声を使って，1回3分から4分程度で終わる問題が，大学入学共通テスト第1回（2021年1月）から第3回（2023年1月）までの過去3年間に渡る英語読解問題に基づいて作成され，合計36題収載されています。このドリルにある簡易テストは，最小英語テスト（The Minimal English Test ＝ MET）と呼びます。時間が最短の英語テストだからです。MET についてのより詳しい説明は，牧秀樹著『The Minimal English Test(最小英語テスト) 研究』（2018年，開拓社）を参考にしてください。

　それよりも，早く音声を聞いて，練習問題をやっていただければ，MET がどんなものか実感できると思います。体験者の声も参考になるかもしれません。

- 頭の中の普段あまり使わないような部分が刺激されている感覚で，最初は聞きとるのに必死だったのが，だんだん意味までわかるようになってきておもしろかった。
- 英語を普段とは違う方法で勉強できておもしろかった。短い時間だったが，リスニング力が上がった感じがして楽しかった。
- この講座を受けた直後，以前はまったく聞きとれなかった音声が聞きとれるようになっていて驚いた。

このドリルが，みなさんの味方となってくれるといいなと願っています。

　本ドリルの英語音声は，クリストファー・ロプレスティ（Christopher LoPresti）氏による録音です。米国バージニア州出身の英語母語話者で，ニューヨーク芸術アカデミーにて芸術修士の学位を得ています。クリストファー・ロプレスティ氏は，実は，マイケル・ロプレスティ（Michael LoPresti）氏の兄で，そのマイケル・ロプレスティ氏は，ウエスト・バージニア州のセイラム帝京大学日本研究学部で私と共に学び，その後，フロリダ州立大学で人口統計学と経済学で修士号を取得しました。現在は，東京大学薬学部医薬政策学講座に在籍し，薬学の博士号取得を目指しています。そして，牧秀樹（2022）『金言版 最小英語テスト（kMET）ドリル』の音声もマイケル・ロプレスティ氏による録音です。

　本ドリルを作成するに当たっては，大学入学共通テスト英語 2021-2023 年読解問題（本試験と追試験）の英文とその音声を利用しています。英文と音声の使用を許可してくださった大学入試センターに心より感謝いたします。また，困難な時世の中，本書の出版を引き受けてくださった開拓社の川田賢氏にも心より感謝いたします。

2024年3月　　牧秀樹・何海希

目　次

MET のやり方

　MET は，英語の音声を聞きながら，単語を埋めるだけの簡単なテストです。音声だけを聞いていれば，それほど速いとは感じませんが，いったんテストが始まると，突然，襲い掛かるように速く感じます。ですから，単語が，聞きとれなかったり，書ききれなかったりした場合は，あきらめて，すぐに，次の空所に移るようにしてください。そうしないと，一度に5つくらい空所が吹っ飛んでしまうことがあり，得点の低下につながってしまいます。

　1題終わるごとに，次のページに日本語訳と解答があるので，答え合わせをしながら，書ききれなかった箇所を確認し，また，意味がわからなかった箇所も，同時に確認してください。日本語訳は，なるべく理解しやすいように，あえて，英文を前から訳しています。英語母語話者は，実際この順番で文の意味を理解していますので，わざわざ，英文で最初の方に現れる動詞を，長い日本文の最後に置かないようにしています。

　本試験18題と追試験18題があります。追試験の方が若干難度が高くなっています。また，各18題は，6題ずつ3つのグループに分かれ，3つのグループは，進むにつれ，難度が上がっています。18題行って，どれだけ自分が伸びたかを測定するには，第1題目の MET を複写しておいて，その第1題目の MET だけは採点せず（つまり，答えを見ず），他の17題が終わってから，その複写した第1題目の MET を行い，そこで，第1題目の MET を2枚，同時に採点してください。何点伸びたかがはっきりわかります。

　それでは，どうぞ，MET で実りの時間を。共通テストの秘密の味方。

大学入学共通テスト本試験版 MET 問題

　この章には，問題が，18 題あります。全問題は，大学入学共通テスト英語本試験の読解テストの過去問題の英文を基に作られているので，MET 2021 本 (1) のように，名前が付けられています。各問題には，空所（　）があります。音声を聞きながら，（　）の中に，英単語を入れてください。18 題は，6 題ずつ 3 つのグループに分かれ，3 つのグループは，進むにつれ，難度が上がっています。

　1 題終わるごとに，答え合わせをすることができます。各問題の次のページには，その英文の日本語訳が，そして，その次のページには，解答が太字で示されています。答え合わせが終わったら，問題のページに戻り，点数を記入しておくことができます。

　まずは，次のページにある練習問題から始めてみましょう。どんな作業をするかわかります。

MET 練習問題

／5 点

英語の音声を聞きながら，（　）の中に，英単語を入れてください。

We're almost at the top of the mountain. Whew! I hope there's a nice
(　　　)[1]. There's a view of the valley and a small lake. It's beautiful.
Great! I want (　　　)[2] get a good picture. It's such a nice morning. I'm
sure the view (　　　)[3] be clear. Ah, here we are. Oh, no! Where's the
valley? There's too much fog. We can't (　　　)[4] anything. Well, let's
have some lunch first. Maybe the fog will clear later. OK. Let's do that.
What did (　　　)[5] bring for lunch? Oh, I thought you brought our
lunch.

MET 練習問題 日本語訳

問題英文の日本語訳を確認しよう。

もうすぐ山頂だね。ふぅ！ いい景色が見られるといいね。谷と小さな湖が見える。きれいだ。いいねえ！ いい写真が撮りたいな。素敵な朝だ。きっと視界が晴れるよ。さあ，着いた。あれまあ！谷はどこだろう？ 霧が多すぎ。何も見えないな。じゃあ，先にお昼にしよう。霧はそのうち晴れるよ。そうだね。そうしよう。昼食に何を持ってきたの？ あら，私たちのお弁当も持ってきてくれてるって思ってた。

MET 練習問題 解答

解答付き英文を見ながら，英語の音声をもう一度聞いてみよう。

We're almost at the top of the mountain. Whew! I hope there's a nice (**view**)[1]. There's a view of the valley and a small lake. It's beautiful. Great! I want (**to**)[2] get a good picture. It's such a nice morning. I'm sure the view (**will**)[3] be clear. Ah, here we are. Oh, no! Where's the valley? There's too much fog. We can't (**see**)[4] anything. Well, let's have some lunch first. Maybe the fog will clear later. OK. Let's do that. What did (**you**)[5] bring for lunch? Oh, I thought you brought our lunch.

MET 2021 本 (1)

英語の音声を聞きながら，（　　）の中に，英単語を入れてください。

Five years ago, Mrs. Sabine Rouas lost her horse. She had spent 20 years with (　　　　　)[1] horse before he died of old age. At (　　　　　)[2] time, she felt that she could never own another horse. (　　　　　)[3] of loneliness, she spent hours watching cows on a nearby milk (　　　　　)[4]. Then, one day, she asked the farmer if she could (　　　　　)[5] look after them. The farmer agreed, and Sabine started work. She quickly developed (　　　　　)[6] friendship with one of the cows. As the (　　　　　)[7] was pregnant, she spent more time with it (　　　　　)[8] with the others. After the cow's baby was born, (　　　　　)[9] baby started following Sabine around. Unfortunately, the farmer wasn't interested in keeping a bull—a male (　　　　　)[10]—on a milk farm. The farmer planned to sell (　　　　　)[11] baby bull, which he called Three-oh-nine (309), to a meat market. Sabine decided (　　　　　)[12] wasn't going to let that happen, so she asked the farmer (　　　　　)[13] she could buy him and his mother. The farmer agreed, (　　　　　)[14] she bought them. Sabine then started taking 309 for walks to town. About nine months later, (　　　　　)[15] at last she had permission to move (　　　　　)[16] animals, they moved to Sabine's farm. Soon after, Sabine was offered a (　　　　　)[17]. At first, she wasn't sure if she wanted to (　　　　　)[18] him, but the memory of her horse was (　　　　　)[19] longer painful, so she accepted the pony and named him Leon. (　　　　　)[20] then decided to return to her old hobby and started training (　　　　　)[21] for show jumping. Three-oh-nine, who she had renamed Aston, spent most (　　　　　)[22] his time with Leon, and the two became really close friends. However, Sabine had

（　　　　）²³ expected Aston to pay close attention to her training routine with Leon, nor （　　　　）²⁴ she expected Aston to pick up some tricks. The young （　　　　）²⁵ quickly mastered walking, galloping, stopping, going backwards, and turning around on command. He responded to Sabine's voice just like （　　　　）²⁶ horse. And despite weighing 1,300 kg, it took him just 18 months to learn （　　　　）²⁷ to leap over one-meter-high horse jumps with Sabine on his （　　　　）²⁸.

MET 2021 本 (1) 日本語訳

問題英文の日本語訳を確認しよう。

5 年前，サビーヌ・ルアス夫人は愛馬を亡くした。彼女は 20 年間をこの馬とともに過ごした。馬が老衰で亡くなるまで。その時，彼女はこう感じた。もう他の馬を飼うことはできないと。寂しさから，彼女は，何時間も過ごした。近くの農場で牛を見ながら。そんなある日，彼女は農場主に牛の世話を手伝ってもいいかと尋ねた。農場主は同意し，サビーヌは仕事を始めた。彼女はすぐに 1 頭の牛と仲良くなった。その牛は妊娠していたので，彼女は，他の牛よりも長い時間いっしょに過ごした。生まれると，その牛の赤ちゃんは，サビーヌの後を追いかけ始めた。残念ながら，その農場主は，雄牛を農場で飼うことには興味がなかった。農場主は，この子牛をスリーオーナイン（309）と名付け，食肉市場に売る計画を立てていた。サビーヌはこれを許してはいけないと思い，農場主にこの子牛と母親を買い取ることができないか尋ねた。農場主は同意し，彼女は，牛の親子を購入した。そして，サビーヌは 309 番を連れて，町に散歩に行き始めた。約 9 か月後，ついに彼女は，この牛の親子を引っ越しさせる許可を得て，結果的に，この牛の親子は，サビーヌの農場に移動した。その直後に，サビーヌはポニーを 1 頭もらうことになった。初めは，ポニーを飼いたいかどうか迷っていたが，かつての馬との思い出は，もはや苦痛ではなくなったので，彼女はポニーを譲り受け，レオンと名付けた。その後，彼女は昔の趣味に戻ることを決意し，レオンに曲馬のトレーニングを始めた。彼女は，スリーオーナインをアストンと改名した。アストンは，ほとんどの時間をレオンと一緒に過ごし，二頭は本当に仲良くなった。しかしながら，サビーヌは，アストンが自分とレオンとのトレーニングをじっと見ているとは予想していなかったし，アストンが技をいくつか習得するとも予想していなかった。この若い雄牛は，命令に応じて，歩くこと，疾走すること，止まること，後退すること，向きを変えることをすぐに習得した。アストンは，サビーヌの声に馬のように応えた。そして，体重が 1,300 kg あったにもかかわらず，たった 18 ヵ月で，高さ 1 メートルもある棒を飛び越える方法を習得してしまった。サビーヌを背中に乗せて。

MET 2021 本 (1) 解答

解答付き英文を見ながら，英語の音声をもう一度聞いてみよう。

Five years ago, Mrs. Sabine Rouas lost her horse. She had spent 20 years with (**the**)[1] horse before he died of old age. At (**that**)[2] time, she felt that she could never own another horse. (**Out**)[3] of loneliness, she spent hours watching cows on a nearby milk (**farm**)[4]. Then, one day, she asked the farmer if she could (**help**)[5] look after them. The farmer agreed, and Sabine started work. She quickly developed (**a**)[6] friendship with one of the cows. As the (**cow**)[7] was pregnant, she spent more time with it (**than**)[8] with the others. After the cow's baby was born, (**the**)[9] baby started following Sabine around. Unfortunately, the farmer wasn't interested in keeping a bull—a male (**cow**)[10]—on a milk farm. The farmer planned to sell (**the**)[11] baby bull, which he called Three-oh-nine (309), to a meat market. Sabine decided (**she**)[12] wasn't going to let that happen, so she asked the farmer (**if**)[13] she could buy him and his mother. The farmer agreed, (**and**)[14] she bought them. Sabine then started taking 309 for walks to town. About nine months later, (**when**)[15] at last she had permission to move (**the**)[16] animals, they moved to Sabine's farm. Soon after, Sabine was offered a (**pony**)[17]. At first, she wasn't sure if she wanted to (**have**)[18] him, but the memory of her horse was (**no**)[19] longer painful, so she accepted the pony and named him Leon. (**She**)[20] then decided to return to her old hobby and started training (**him**)[21] for show jumping. Three-oh-nine, who she had renamed Aston, spent most (**of**)[22] his time with Leon, and the two became really close friends. However, Sabine had (**not**)[23] expected Aston to pay close attention to her training routine with Leon, nor (**had**)[24] she expected Aston to pick up some tricks. The young (**bull**)[25] quickly mastered walking, galloping, stopping, going backwards, and turning around on command. He responded to Sabine's voice just like (**a**)[26] horse. And despite weighing 1,300 kg, it took him just 18 months to learn (**how**)[27] to leap over one-meter-high horse jumps with Sabine on his (**back**)[28].

MET 2021 本 (2)

英語の音声を聞きながら，（　　）の中に，英単語を入れてください。

Aston might never have learned those things without having watched Leon. Moreover, Aston understood distance and could adjust his steps before a jump. He (　　　　)[1] noticed his faults and corrected them without any help from Sabine. That's something (　　　　)[2] the very best Olympic-standard horses can do. Now Sabine (　　　　)[3] Aston go to weekend fairs and horse shows around Europe to show off (　　　　)[4] skills. Sabine says, "We get a good reaction. Mostly, people are really surprised, (　　　　)[5] at first, they can be a bit scared because he's (　　　　)[6]— much bigger than a horse. Most people don't like to (　　　　)[7] too close to bulls with horns. But once they (　　　　)[8] his real nature, and see him performing, they often (　　　　)[9], 'Oh he's really quite beautiful.'" "Look!" And Sabine shows a photo of Aston on her smartphone. (　　　　)[10] then continues, "When Aston was very young, I used (　　　　)[11] take him out for walks on a (　　　　)[12], like a dog, so that he would (　　　　)[13] used to humans. Maybe that's why he doesn't mind people. Because he (　　　　)[14] so calm, children, in particular, really like watching him and getting (　　　　)[15] chance to be close to him." Over the (　　　　)[16] few years, news of the massive show-jumping bull has spread rapidly; (　　　　)[17], Aston is a major attraction with a growing number of online followers. Aston and Sabine sometimes (　　　　)[18] to travel 200 or 300 kilometers away from home, which means they (　　　　)[19] to stay overnight. Aston has to sleep in a horse (　　　　)[20], which isn't really big enough for him. "He doesn't like it. (　　　　)[21] have to sleep with him in the (   )²²," says Sabine.   "But you know, when he wakes

(   )²³ and changes position, he is very careful not to crush

(   )²⁴. He really is very gentle.   He sometimes gets lonely, and

(   )²⁵ doesn't like being away from Leon for too long; (   )²⁶

other than that, he's very happy."

MET 2021 本（2）日本語訳

問題英文の日本語訳を確認しよう。

アストンは，レオンを見ずには，それらのことを学ぶことはできなかったかもしれない。さらにアストンは，距離を理解し，ジャンプする前に歩幅を調整することができた。アストンはまた，自分の欠点に気づき，サビーヌの助けなしに修正した。それはオリンピック基準の最高の馬だけができることだ。現在，サビーヌとアストンは，ヨーロッパ中の週末の見本市や馬のショーに出かけて，そのスキルを披露している。サビーヌはこう言う。「反応はいいですよ。ほとんどの場合，人々は本当に驚きます。初めは，少し怖がるかもしれません。だって，アストンは馬よりはるかに大きいんだから。ほとんどの人は角のある雄牛に近づきたがりません。でも，いったんアストンの本当の性質を見て，そのパフォーマンスを見たら，人は，こう言いますよ。『ああ，この牛は，本当に美しい』」「見て！」と，サビーヌはスマートフォンでアストンの写真を見せてくれる。さらに彼女はこう続ける。「アストンがまだ幼い頃，犬のようにリードを付けて散歩に連れ出したの。その結果，人間に慣れたんだと思う。だからこそアストンは，人を気にしないのかもしれません。アストンはとても穏やかなので，特に子供たちは，アストンを見るのが大好きで，なんとかアストンに近づこうとしたがるんですよ」ここ数年，曲馬をする巨大な雄牛のニュースが急速に広まった。今や，アストンは，娯楽の目玉で，オンラインのフォロワー数が激増している。アストンとサビーヌは，時々，家から200キロ，300キロ離れたところを旅する必要があり，一晩外で過ごさなければならない。アストンは移動用の馬小屋で寝なければならないが，アストンにとっては十分大きいとは言えない。「アストンはその馬小屋が好きじゃないんです。私はその中でアストンと一緒に寝なければなりません」とサビーヌは言う。「でもね，アストンが目を覚まして体勢を変える時，私を押しつぶさないように細心の注意を払ってくれているんですよ。アストンは本当に優しい。アストンは時々寂しくなるので，レオンと長く離れるのは好きではありません。でもそれ以外は，アストンはとても幸せですよ」

MET 2021 本 (2) 解答

解答付き英文を見ながら，英語の音声をもう一度聞いてみよう。

Aston might never have learned those things without having watched Leon. Moreover, Aston understood distance and could adjust his steps before a jump. He (**also**)[1] noticed his faults and corrected them without any help from Sabine. That's something (**only**)[2] the very best Olympic-standard horses can do. Now Sabine (**and**)[3] Aston go to weekend fairs and horse shows around Europe to show off (**his**)[4] skills. Sabine says, "We get a good reaction. Mostly, people are really surprised, (**and**)[5] at first, they can be a bit scared because he's (**big**)[6]—much bigger than a horse. Most people don't like to (**get**)[7] too close to bulls with horns. But once they (**see**)[8] his real nature, and see him performing, they often (**say**)[9], 'Oh he's really quite beautiful.'" "Look!" And Sabine shows a photo of Aston on her smartphone. (**She**)[10] then continues, "When Aston was very young, I used (**to**)[11] take him out for walks on a (**lead**)[12], like a dog, so that he would (**get**)[13] used to humans. Maybe that's why he doesn't mind people. Because he (**is**)[14] so calm, children, in particular, really like watching him and getting (**a**)[15] chance to be close to him." Over the (**last**)[16] few years, news of the massive show-jumping bull has spread rapidly; (**now**)[17], Aston is a major attraction with a growing number of online followers. Aston and Sabine sometimes (**need**)[18] to travel 200 or 300 kilometers away from home, which means they (**have**)[19] to stay overnight. Aston has to sleep in a horse (**box**)[20], which isn't really big enough for him. "He doesn't like it. (**I**)[21] have to sleep with him in the (**box**)[22]," says Sabine. "But you know, when he wakes (**up**)[23] and changes position, he is very careful not to crush (**me**)[24]. He really is very gentle. He sometimes gets lonely, and (**he**)[25] doesn't like being away from Leon for too long; (**but**)[26] other than that, he's very happy."

MET 2021 本 (3)

英語の音声を聞きながら，（　）の中に，英単語を入れてください。

Ice hockey is a team sport enjoyed by a (　　　)[1] variety of people around the world. The object of the sport is (　　　)[2] move a hard rubber disk called a "puck" into (　　　)[3] other team's net with a hockey stick. Two teams with six players on each (　　　)[4] engage in this fast-paced sport on a hard and slippery (　　　)[5] rink. Players may reach a speed of 30 kilometers per hour sending (　　　)[6] puck into the air. At this (　　　)[7], both the players and the puck can (　　　)[8] a cause of serious danger. The speed of the sport and (　　　)[9] slippery surface of the ice rink make it (　　　)[10] for players to fall down or bump (　　　)[11] each other resulting in a variety of injuries. In an attempt (　　　)[12] protect players, equipment such as helmets, gloves, and pads for the shoulders, elbows, (　　　)[13] legs, has been introduced over the years. Despite these efforts, ice hockey (　　　)[14] a high rate of concussions. A concussion is (　　　)[15] injury to the brain that affects the way it functions; (　　　)[16] is caused by either direct or indirect impact to the head, (　　　)[17], neck, or elsewhere and can sometimes cause temporary loss of consciousness. (　　　)[18] less serious cases, for a short time, players may be unable (　　　)[19] walk straight or see clearly, or they may experience ringing (　　　)[20] the ears. Some believe they just have (　　　)[21] slight headache and do not realize they have injured their brains. In addition (　　　)[22] not realizing the seriousness of the injury, players tend to worry about (　　　)[23] their coach will think. In the past, coaches preferred tough players who played in spite (　　　)[24] the pain.

In other words, while it would seem logical for (   )²⁵ injured player to stop playing after getting hurt, many did not. Recently, however, (   )²⁶ has been found that concussions can have serious effects that (   )²⁷ a lifetime.

MET 2021 本（3）日本語訳

問題英文の日本語訳を確認しよう。

アイスホッケーは，チームスポーツで，世界中のさまざまな人々に楽しまれている。このスポーツの目的は，硬いゴム製の円盤，「パック」と呼ばれているが，それを相手チームのネットに入れることだ。ホッケースティックを使って。2つのチームが，それぞれ，6人のプレーヤーからなるが，このペースの速いスポーツに取り組む。硬くて滑りやすいアイスリンクの上で。プレーヤーは時速30キロメートルの速度に達し，パックを空中に飛ばすことができる。このペースでは，プレーヤーとパックの両方が重大な危険の原因となりうる。このスポーツのスピードとアイスリンクの表面が滑りやすいために，プレーヤーが転んだり，プレーヤー同士がぶつかったりして，さまざまな怪我が発生しやすくなる。プレーヤーを保護するために，安全のための装備が長年にわたって導入されてきた。ヘルメット，グローブ，肩，肘，脚用のパッドなどの。こうした努力にもかかわらず，アイスホッケーでは脳震盪（のうしんとう）の発生率が高い。脳震盪は，脳の機能に影響を及ぼす脳の損傷だ。これは，頭，顔，首などへの直接的または間接的な衝撃によって引き起こされ，時には，一時的な意識喪失を引き起こす場合がある。それほど深刻ではないケースでは，プレーヤーは短時間，まっすぐに歩けなくなったり，はっきりとものが見えなくなったり，耳鳴りを経験したりすることがある。軽い頭痛があるだけだと思ったり，脳が損傷していることに気づかないプレーヤーもいる。怪我の深刻さに気づいていないだけでなく，プレーヤーは，コーチにどう思われるかを心配する傾向がある。かつて，コーチはタフな選手を好んでいた。痛みをものともせずにプレーするような。言い換えれば，怪我をしたプレーヤーが怪我をした後にプレーをやめるのは論理的であるように思えるが，多くのプレーヤーは，プレーをやめなかった。しかしながら，最近になって，脳震盪は，生涯続くような深刻な影響をもたらしうることがわかってきた。

MET 2021 本 (3) 解答

解答付き英文を見ながら，英語の音声をもう一度聞いてみよう。

Ice hockey is a team sport enjoyed by a (**wide**)[1] variety of people around the world. The object of the sport is (**to**)[2] move a hard rubber disk called a "puck" into (**the**)[3] other team's net with a hockey stick. Two teams with six players on each (**team**)[4] engage in this fast-paced sport on a hard and slippery (**ice**)[5] rink. Players may reach a speed of 30 kilometers per hour sending (**the**)[6] puck into the air. At this (**pace**)[7], both the players and the puck can (**be**)[8] a cause of serious danger. The speed of the sport and (**the**)[9] slippery surface of the ice rink make it (**easy**)[10] for players to fall down or bump (**into**)[11] each other resulting in a variety of injuries. In an attempt (**to**)[12] protect players, equipment such as helmets, gloves, and pads for the shoulders, elbows, (**and**)[13] legs, has been introduced over the years. Despite these efforts, ice hockey (**has**)[14] a high rate of concussions. A concussion is (**an**)[15] injury to the brain that affects the way it functions; (**it**)[16] is caused by either direct or indirect impact to the head, (**face**)[17], neck, or elsewhere and can sometimes cause temporary loss of consciousness. (**In**)[18] less serious cases, for a short time, players may be unable (**to**)[19] walk straight or see clearly, or they may experience ringing (**in**)[20] the ears. Some believe they just have (**a**)[21] slight headache and do not realize they have injured their brains. In addition (**to**)[22] not realizing the seriousness of the injury, players tend to worry about (**what**)[23] their coach will think. In the past, coaches preferred tough players who played in spite (**of**)[24] the pain. In other words, while it would seem logical for (**an**)[25] injured player to stop playing after getting hurt, many did not. Recently, however, (**it**)[26] has been found that concussions can have serious effects that (**last**)[27] a lifetime.

MET 2021 本 (4)

英語の音声を聞きながら, (   ) の中に, 英単語を入れてください。

People with a history of concussion may have trouble concentrating or sleeping. Moreover, (   )[1] may suffer from psychological problems such as depression and mood changes. (   )[2] some cases, players may develop smell and taste disorders. The National Hockey League (NHL), consisting of teams in Canada (   )[3] the United States, has been making stricter rules and guidelines to deal (   )[4] concussions. For example, in 2001, the NHL introduced the wearing of visors-pieces of clear plastic attached (   )[5] the helmet that protect the face. At first, it (   )[6] optional and many players chose not to wear them. Since 2013, however, (   )[7] has been required. In addition, in 2004, the NHL began to (   )[8] more severe penalties, such as suspensions and fines, to players who (   )[9] another player in the head deliberately. The NHL also introduced a concussion spotters system (   )[10] 2015. In this system, NHL officials with access to live streaming and video replay watch (   )[11] visible indications of concussion during each game. At first, two concussion spotters, who had (   )[12] medical training, monitored the game in the arena. The following year, one (   )[13] four concussion spotters with medical training were added. They monitored each game from (   )[14] League's head office in New York. If a spotter thinks that a player (   )[15] suffered a concussion, the player is removed from the game (   )[16] is taken to a "quiet (room)" for an examination (   )[17] a medical doctor. The player is not allowed to return to (   )[18] game until the doctor gives permission. The NHL has made much progress (   )[19] making ice hockey a safer sport. As more is learned about the causes (   )[20] effects of concussions, the NHL will surely take further measures to ensure player safety. Better safety might lead (   )[21] an increase in the number of ice hockey players and (   )[22].

MET 2021 本（4）日本語訳

問題英文の日本語訳を確認しよう。

脳震盪（のうしんとう）の経験がある人には，集中力や睡眠に問題がありうる。さらに，心理的問題に悩まされることもある。うつ病や気分の変化などの。場合によっては，プレーヤーが嗅覚障害や味覚障害を発症する可能性もある。ナショナルホッケーリーグ（NHL）は，カナダと米国のチームで構成されているが，ルールとガイドラインを厳格化している。脳震盪に対処するために。例えば，2001 年に，NHL は，透明なプラスチック製のバイザーの着用を導入した。それは，顔を保護するヘルメットに取り付けられている。初めは，これはオプションで，多くのプレーヤーは着用しなかった。しかしながら，2013 年以降は，着用が義務化された。さらに 2004 年，NHL は，より厳しい罰則を与えるようになった。故意に他の選手の頭を殴った選手に対して。それは，出場停止や罰金などの罰則である。NHL は 2015 年に，脳震盪監視システムも導入した。このシステムでは，NHL 関係者で，ライブストリーミングとビデオリプレイを見ることができる関係者が，各試合中に，目に見える脳震盪の兆候を監視する。初めは，医療訓練を受けていない脳震盪監視員が 2 人，アリーナで試合を監視していた。翌年，医学的訓練を受けた脳震盪監視員が 1 人から 4 人追加された。脳震盪監視員は，ニューヨークにあるリーグ本部から各試合を監視した。プレーヤーが脳震盪を起こしたと脳震盪監視員が判断した場合，プレーヤーはゲームから外され，「安静室」に連れて行かれる。医師による検査のために。プレーヤーは，医師の許可が出るまで，ゲームに戻れない。NHL は，大きな進歩を遂げてきた。アイスホッケーをより安全なスポーツにするために。脳震盪の原因と影響についてさらに解明されるにつれ，NHL がさらなる措置を講じることは確実だ。選手の安全を確保するために。安全性の向上は，アイスホッケー選手やファンの数の増加につながるだろう。

MET 2021 本 (4) 解答

解答付き英文を見ながら，英語の音声をもう一度聞いてみよう。

People with a history of concussion may have trouble concentrating or sleeping. Moreover, (**they**)[1] may suffer from psychological problems such as depression and mood changes. (**In**)[2] some cases, players may develop smell and taste disorders. The National Hockey League (NHL), consisting of teams in Canada (**and**)[3] the United States, has been making stricter rules and guidelines to deal (**with**)[4] concussions. For example, in 2001, the NHL introduced the wearing of visors-pieces of clear plastic attached (**to**)[5] the helmet that protect the face. At first, it (**was**)[6] optional and many players chose not to wear them. Since 2013, however, (**it**)[7] has been required. In addition, in 2004, the NHL began to (**give**)[8] more severe penalties, such as suspensions and fines, to players who (**hit**)[9] another player in the head deliberately. The NHL also introduced a concussion spotters system (**in**)[10] 2015. In this system, NHL officials with access to live streaming and video replay watch (**for**)[11] visible indications of concussion during each game. At first, two concussion spotters, who had (**no**)[12] medical training, monitored the game in the arena. The following year, one (**to**)[13] four concussion spotters with medical training were added. They monitored each game from (**the**)[14] League's head office in New York. If a spotter thinks that a player (**has**)[15] suffered a concussion, the player is removed from the game (**and**)[16] is taken to a "quiet (**room**)" for an examination (**by**)[17] a medical doctor. The player is not allowed to return to (**the**)[18] game until the doctor gives permission. The NHL has made much progress (**in**)[19] making ice hockey a safer sport. As more is learned about the causes (**and**)[20] effects of concussions, the NHL will surely take further measures to ensure player safety. Better safety might lead (**to**)[21] an increase in the number of ice hockey players and (**fans**)[22].

MET 2021 本 (5)

英語の音声を聞きながら，（　　）の中に，英単語を入れてください。

Cake, candy, soft drinks—most of us love sweet things. (　　　　)[1] fact, young people say "Sweet!" to mean something is "good" (　　　　)[2] English. When we think of sweetness, we imagine ordinary white sugar from sugar cane (　　　　)[3] sugar beet plants. Scientific discoveries, however, have changed the world of sweeteners. We can (　　　　)[4] extract sugars from many other plants. The most obvious example is corn. (　　　　)[5] is abundant, inexpensive, and easy to process. High fructose corn syrup (HFCS) (　　　　)[6] about 1.2 times sweeter than regular sugar, but quite high in calories. Taking science one step further, over (　　　　)[7] past 70 years scientists have developed a wide variety of artificial sweeteners. A recent US National Health and Nutrition Examination Survey concluded (　　　　)[8] 14.6% of the average American's energy intake is from "added sugar," which refers to sugar that (　　　　)[9] not derived from whole foods. A banana, for example, is a whole (　　　　)[10], while a cookie contains added sugar. More than half of added sugar calories are (　　　　)[11] sweetened drinks and desserts. Lots of added sugar can have negative effects on (　　　　)[12] bodies, including excessive weight gain and other health problems. For this reason, many choose low-calorie substitutes for drinks, snacks, (　　　　)[13] desserts. Natural alternatives to white sugar include brown sugar, honey, and maple syrup, but they also tend (　　　　)[14] be high in calories. Consequently, alternative "low-calorie sweeteners" (LCSs), mostly artificial chemical combinations, have become popular. The most common LCSs today (　　　　)[15] aspartame, Ace-K, stevia, and sucralose. Not all LCSs are artificial—stevia comes from plant leaves. Alternative sweeteners can (　　　　)[16] hard to use in cooking because some cannot be heated (　　　　)[17] most are far sweeter than white sugar.

MET 2021 本 (5) 日本語訳

問題英文の日本語訳を確認しよう。

ケーキ，キャンディー，ソフトドリンクなど，私たちのほとんどは，甘いものが大好きだ。実際，若者は「あまーーい」と言う。英語で何かが「いい」という意味で。甘味と言うと，サトウキビやテンサイからとれる普通の白砂糖を想像する。しかし，科学的な発見は甘味料の世界を変えた。今では他の多くの植物からも糖を抽出できるようになった。最もわかりやすい例は，トウモロコシだ。トウモロコシは豊富にあり，安価で加工が簡単だ。高果糖コーンシロップ（HFCS）は，通常の砂糖より約 1.2 倍甘いが，カロリーはかなり高い。科学をさらに一歩進めて，過去 70 年にわたり，科学者はさまざまな人工甘味料を開発してきた。最近の米国国民健康栄養調査は，次のように結論付けている。平均的なアメリカ人のエネルギー摂取量の 14.6% が「添加糖」からのものである。これは，自然食品由来ではない砂糖を指している。例えば，バナナは自然食品であるが，クッキーには砂糖が添加されている。追加される砂糖のカロリーの半分以上は，甘い飲み物やデザートからのものだ。砂糖を大量に添加すると，私たちの体に悪影響を与える可能性がある。過度の体重増加やその他の健康上の問題など。このため，多くの人は，低カロリーの代替品を選ぶ。飲み物，スナック，デザートに。白砂糖の自然の代替品には，黒砂糖，蜂蜜，メープルシロップなどがあるが，これらもカロリーが高い傾向がある。その結果，代替の「低カロリー甘味料」（LCS），主に人工化学物質を組み合わせたもの，が普及してきた。現在，最も一般的な LCS は，アスパルテーム，Ace-K，ステビア，および，スクラロースだ。必ずしもすべての LCS が人工物というわけではない。ステビアは，植物の葉由来だ。料理に使いにくい代替甘味料もある。加熱できないものがあったり，ほとんどが白砂糖よりはるかに甘いからだ。

MET 2021 本 (5) 解答

解答付き英文を見ながら，英語の音声をもう一度聞いてみよう。

Cake, candy, soft drinks—most of us love sweet things. (**In**)[1] fact, young people say "Sweet!" to mean something is "good" (**in**)[2] English. When we think of sweetness, we imagine ordinary white sugar from sugar cane (**or**)[3] sugar beet plants. Scientific discoveries, however, have changed the world of sweeteners. We can (**now**)[4] extract sugars from many other plants. The most obvious example is corn. (**Corn**)[5] is abundant, inexpensive, and easy to process. High fructose corn syrup (HFCS) (**is**)[6] about 1.2 times sweeter than regular sugar, but quite high in calories. Taking science one step further, over (**the**)[7] past 70 years scientists have developed a wide variety of artificial sweeteners. A recent US National Health and Nutrition Examination Survey concluded (**that**)[8] 14.6% of the average American's energy intake is from "added sugar," which refers to sugar that (**is**)[9] not derived from whole foods. A banana, for example, is a whole (**food**)[10], while a cookie contains added sugar. More than half of added sugar calories are (**from**)[11] sweetened drinks and desserts. Lots of added sugar can have negative effects on (**our**)[12] bodies, including excessive weight gain and other health problems. For this reason, many choose low-calorie substitutes for drinks, snacks, (**and**)[13] desserts. Natural alternatives to white sugar include brown sugar, honey, and maple syrup, but they also tend (**to**)[14] be high in calories. Consequently, alternative "low-calorie sweeteners" (LCSs), mostly artificial chemical combinations, have become popular. The most common LCSs today (**are**)[15] aspartame, Ace-K, stevia, and sucralose. Not all LCSs are artificial—stevia comes from plant leaves. Alternative sweeteners can (**be**)[16] hard to use in cooking because some cannot be heated (**and**)[17] most are far sweeter than white sugar.

英語の音声を聞きながら，（　）の中に，英単語を入れてください。

Aspartame and Ace-K are 200 times sweeter than sugar. Stevia is 300 times sweeter, and sucralose has twice (　　　)[1] sweetness of stevia. Some new sweeteners are even more intense. (　　　)[2] Japanese company recently developed "Adventure," which is 20,000 times sweeter than sugar. Only a tiny amount of (　　　)[3] substance is required to sweeten something. When choosing sweeteners, it is important to consider health issues. Making desserts (　　　)[4] lots of white sugar, for example, results in high-calorie dishes that could lead (　　　)[5] weight gain. There are those who prefer LCSs for this very reason. Apart (　　　)[6] calories, however, some research links consuming artificial LCSs with various other health concerns. Some LCSs contain strong chemicals suspected of causing cancer, while others have been shown (　　　)[7] affect memory and brain development, so they can be dangerous, especially for young children, pregnant women, (　　　)[8] the elderly. There are a few relatively natural alternative sweeteners, like xylitol and sorbitol, which (　　　)[9] low in calories. Unfortunately, these move through the body extremely slowly, so consuming large amounts (　　　)[10] cause stomach trouble. When people want something sweet, even with all the information, (　　　)[11] is difficult for them to decide whether to stick to common higher calorie sweeteners (　　　)[12] sugar or to use LCSs. Many varieties of gum (　　　)[13] candy today contain one or more artificial sweeteners; nonetheless, some people who would not put artificial sweeteners (　　　)[14] hot drinks may still buy such items. Individuals need to weigh (　　　)[15] options and then choose the sweeteners that best suit their needs (　　　)[16] circumstances.

27

MET 2021 本 (6) 日本語訳

問題英文の日本語訳を確認しよう。

アスパルテームと Ace-K は，砂糖の 200 倍甘い。ステビアは，砂糖の 300 倍甘く，スクラロースはステビアの 2 倍甘い。新しい甘味料の中には，さらに強力なものもある。最近，日本の企業が「アドベンチャー」を開発した。これは，砂糖の 2 万倍の甘さを持っている。この物質がほんの少量あれば，何かを甘くすることができる。甘味料を選ぶ時は，健康問題を考慮することが重要だ。例えば，白砂糖をたくさん使ってデザートを作ると，高カロリーの料理になり，体重増加につながる可能性がある。まさにこの理由で LCS を好む人もいる。しかしながら，カロリーとは別に，人工 LCS の摂取とその他のさまざまな健康上の懸念を結びつける研究もある。LCS の中には，強力な化学物質で，発がん性が疑われるもの，が含まれているものもある。また，記憶や脳の発達に影響を与えることがわかっているものもある。特に幼児，妊婦，高齢者にとって危険性が高いものだ。比較的天然の代替甘味料もいくつかある。キシリトールやソルビトールなどだ。これらは，低カロリーだ。残念ながら，これらは体内を非常にゆっくりと移動するため，大量に摂取すると，胃の問題を引き起こす可能性がある。甘いものが欲しい時，あらゆる情報があっても，決断するのは，困難だ。砂糖などの一般的な高カロリー甘味料を使用するか，LCS を使用するか。今日，多くの種類のガムやキャンディには 1 つ以上の人工甘味料が含まれている。それにもかかわらず，温かい飲み物には人工甘味料を入れたくないのに，ガムやキャンディのような商品を購入する人もいるかもしれない。個々人は，目の前の選択肢を比較検討し，甘味料を選択する必要がある。自分のニーズと状況に最も適した甘味料である。

MET 2021 本 (6) 解答

解答付き英文を見ながら，英語の音声をもう一度聞いてみよう。

Aspartame and Ace-K are 200 times sweeter than sugar. Stevia is 300 times sweeter, and sucralose has twice (**the**)[1] sweetness of stevia. Some new sweeteners are even more intense. (**A**)[2] Japanese company recently developed "Adventure," which is 20,000 times sweeter than sugar. Only a tiny amount of (**this**)[3] substance is required to sweeten something. When choosing sweeteners, it is important to consider health issues. Making desserts (**with**)[4] lots of white sugar, for example, results in high-calorie dishes that could lead (**to**)[5] weight gain. There are those who prefer LCSs for this very reason. Apart (**from**)[6] calories, however, some research links consuming artificial LCSs with various other health concerns. Some LCSs contain strong chemicals suspected of causing cancer, while others have been shown (**to**)[7] affect memory and brain development, so they can be dangerous, especially for young children, pregnant women, (**and**)[8] the elderly. There are a few relatively natural alternative sweeteners, like xylitol and sorbitol, which (**are**)[9] low in calories. Unfortunately, these move through the body extremely slowly, so consuming large amounts (**can**)[10] cause stomach trouble. When people want something sweet, even with all the information, (**it**)[11] is difficult for them to decide whether to stick to common higher calorie sweeteners (**like**)[12] sugar or to use LCSs. Many varieties of gum (**and**)[13] candy today contain one or more artificial sweeteners; nonetheless, some people who would not put artificial sweeteners (**in**)[14] hot drinks may still buy such items. Individuals need to weigh (**the**)[15] options and then choose the sweeteners that best suit their needs (**and**)[16] circumstances.

MET 2022 本 (1)

英語の音声を聞きながら，（　　）の中に，英単語を入れてください。

Who invented television? It is not an (　　　　　)[1] question to answer. In the early years of the 20th century, there (　　　　)[2] something called a mechanical television system, but it was not (　　　　)[3] success. Inventors were also competing to develop an electronic television system, which later became the basis (　　　　)[4] what we have today. In the US, there (　　　　)[5] a battle over the patent for the electronic television system, which attracted people's attention because (　　　　)[6] was between a young man and a giant corporation. (　　　　)[7] patent would give the inventor the official right to be (　　　　)[8] only person to develop, use, or sell (　　　　)[9] system. Philo Taylor Farnsworth was born in a log cabin (　　　　)[10] Utah in 1906. His family did not have electricity until (　　　　)[11] was 12 years old, and he was excited (　　　　)[12] find a generator—a machine that produces electricity—when (　　　　)[13] moved into a new home. He (　　　　)[14] very interested in mechanical and electrical technology, reading any information he could (　　　　)[15] on the subject. He would often repair the old generator (　　　　)[16] even changed his mother's hand-powered washing machine into an electricity-powered one. One day, while working (　　　　)[17] his father's potato field, he looked behind him and saw (　　　　)[18] the straight parallel rows of soil that (　　　　)[19] had made. Suddenly, it occurred to him (　　　　)[20] it might be possible to create an electronic image on (　　　　)[21] screen using parallel lines, just like the rows in (　　　　)[22] field. In 1922, during the spring semester of his first year (　　　　)[23] high school, he presented this idea to (   )²⁴ chemistry teacher, Justin Tolman, and asked for advice about his concept of an electronic television system. (   )²⁵ sketches and diagrams on blackboards, he showed the teacher how (   )²⁶ might be accomplished, and Tolman encouraged him to develop his ideas. (   )²⁷ September 7, 1927, Farnsworth succeeded in sending his first electronic image.

MET 2022 本 (1) 日本語訳

問題英文の日本語訳を確認しよう。

テレビを発明したのは誰か？ 答えるのが簡単な質問ではない。20 世紀初頭には，機械式テレビシステムと呼ばれるものがあったが，成功しなかった。発明家たちはまた，電子テレビシステムの開発も競い合った。それは，後に今日私たちが持っているものの基礎となったものだ。米国では，電子テレビシステムの特許を巡る争いがあり，注目を集めた。というのも，それが若者と巨大企業の間で争われたからだ。この特許は，その発明者に，正式な権利を与えるようなものだった。この特許があれば，唯一の人物として，システムを開発，使用，または販売することができるのだ。ファイロ・テイラー・ファーンズワースは，1906 年にユタ州の丸太小屋で生まれた。彼の家には，彼が 12 歳になるまで電気がなかった。彼は，発電機（電気を発生させる機械）を見つけて興奮した。新しい家に引っ越した時に。彼は機械技術と電気技術に非常に興味を持っており，あらゆる情報を読んだ。そのテーマに関して見つけられうるあらゆる情報だ。彼は古い発電機を頻繁に修理し，母親の手動の洗濯機を電気で動く洗濯機に作り変えたこともあった。ある日，父親のジャガイモ畑で働いている時に，後ろを振り返ると，自分が作った畝（うね）がまっすぐに平行に並んでいるのが見えた。突然，彼は思いついた。平行線を使用してスクリーン上に電子画像を作成できるかもしれない。この畑の列と同じように。1922 年，高校 1 年の春学期中に，彼はこのアイデアを化学教師のジャスティン・トールマンに提示し，電子テレビシステムの概念についてアドバイスを求めた。彼は黒板にスケッチや図を書き，それをどのように実現できるかを教師に示し，トールマンは，アイデアを発展させるよう励ました。1927 年 9 月 7 日，ファーンズワースは最初の電子画像の送信に成功した。

MET 2022 本（1）解答

解答付き英文を見ながら，英語の音声をもう一度聞いてみよう。

Who invented television? It is not an (**easy**)[1] question to answer. In the early years of the 20th century, there (**was**)[2] something called a mechanical television system, but it was not (**a**)[3] success. Inventors were also competing to develop an electronic television system, which later became the basis (**of**)[4] what we have today. In the US, there (**was**)[5] a battle over the patent for the electronic television system, which attracted people's attention because (**it**)[6] was between a young man and a giant corporation. (**This**)[7] patent would give the inventor the official right to be (**the**)[8] only person to develop, use, or sell (**the**)[9] system. Philo Taylor Farnsworth was born in a log cabin (**in**)[10] Utah in 1906. His family did not have electricity until (**he**)[11] was 12 years old, and he was excited (**to**)[12] find a generator—a machine that produces electricity—when (**they**)[13] moved into a new home. He (**was**)[14] very interested in mechanical and electrical technology, reading any information he could (**find**)[15] on the subject. He would often repair the old generator (**and**)[16] even changed his mother's hand-powered washing machine into an electricity-powered one. One day, while working (**in**)[17] his father's potato field, he looked behind him and saw (**all**)[18] the straight parallel rows of soil that (**he**)[19] had made. Suddenly, it occurred to him (**that**)[20] it might be possible to create an electronic image on (**a**)[21] screen using parallel lines, just like the rows in (**the**)[22] field. In 1922, during the spring semester of his first year (**at**)[23] high school, he presented this idea to (**his**)[24] chemistry teacher, Justin Tolman, and asked for advice about his concept of an electronic television system. (**With**)[25] sketches and diagrams on blackboards, he showed the teacher how (**it**)[26] might be accomplished, and Tolman encouraged him to develop his ideas. (**On**)[27] September 7, 1927, Farnsworth succeeded in sending his first electronic image.

MET 2022 本 (2)

英語の音声を聞きながら，（　　）の中に，英単語を入れてください。

In the following years, he further improved the system so (　　　　)[1] it could successfully broadcast live images. The US government gave him (　　　　)[2] patent for this system in 1930. However, Farnsworth was not (　　　　)[3] only one working on such a system. A giant company, RCA (Radio Corporation of America), (　　　　)[4] saw a bright future for television and did (　　　　)[5] want to miss the opportunity. They recruited Vladimir Zworykin, (　　　　)[6] had already worked on an electronic television system and had earned (　　　　)[7] patent as early as 1923. Yet, in 1931, they offered Farnsworth (　　　　)[8] large sum of money to sell them (　　　　)[9] patent as his system was superior to that (　　　　)[10] Zworykin's. He refused this offer, which started a patent war between Farnsworth and RCA. (　　　　)[11] company took legal action against Farnsworth, claiming that Zworykin's 1923 patent had priority even though he (　　　　)[12] never made a working version of his system. Farnsworth lost (　　　　)[13] first two rounds of the court case. However, in the final round, (　　　　)[14] teacher who had copied Farnsworth's blackboard drawings gave evidence that Farnsworth did (　　　　)[15] the idea of an electronic television system at least (　　　　)[16] year before Zworykin's patent was issued. In 1934, a judge approved Farnsworth's patent claim on (　　　　)[17] strength of handwritten notes made by his old (　　　　)[18] school teacher, Tolman. Farnsworth died in 1971 at the age (　　　　)[19] 64. He held about 300 US and foreign patents, mostly in radio and television, (　　　　)[20] in 1999, TIME magazine included Farnsworth in Time

100: The Most Important People of the Century. In an interview after his death, Farnsworth's (   )^{21} Pem recalled Neil Armstrong's moon landing being broadcast. Watching the television with her, Farnsworth had (   )^{22}, "Pem, this has made it all worthwhile." (   )^{23} story will always be tied to his teenage dream (   )^{24} sending moving pictures through the air and those blackboard drawings at his (   )^{25} school.

MET 2022 本（2）日本語訳

問題英文の日本語訳を確認しよう。

その後数年で，ファーンズワースはシステムをさらに改良し，ライブ画像を正常に放送できるようにした。米国政府は 1930 年にファーンズワースにこのシステムの特許を与えた。しかし，このようなシステムに取り組んでいたのは，ファーンズワースだけではなかった。巨大企業 RCA（Radio Corporation of America）もテレビの明るい未来を見据え，この機会を逃すまいとしていた。彼らは，ウラジミール・ズウォリキンを採用した。彼は，すでに電子テレビシステムに取り組んでおり，1923 年にはすでに特許を取得していた。それでも 1931 年に，彼らは，ファンズワースに多額の金銭と引き換えに，その特許を売却しれくれるよう懇願した。というのも，彼のシステムがズウォリキンのよりも優れていたからだ。ファンズワースはこの申し出を拒否し，これによりファーンズワースと RCA の間で特許戦争が始まった。同社はファーンズワースに対し訴訟を起こした。ズウォリキンの 1923 年の特許に優先権があると主張して。もっとも，ズウォリキンがシステムの実用バージョンを一度も作ったことがなかったにもかかわらず。ファーンズワースは訴訟の最初の 2 回で敗訴した。しかし，最終回で，例の教師が，証拠を示した。その教師は，ファーンズワースの黒板の絵をコピーし，次の証拠を示した。それは，ファーンズワースが電子テレビシステムのアイデアを最初に持っており，それは，ズウォリキンの特許が発行される少なくとも 1 年前であったという証拠である。1934 年，裁判官は，ファンズワースの特許請求を承認した。ファーンズワースの高校時代の教師トールマンが作成した手書きのメモを根拠に。ファーンズワースは 1971 年に 64 歳で亡くなった。彼は主にラジオとテレビに関する特許を国内外で約 300 件取得していた。1999 年にはタイム誌の「タイム 100：今世紀で最も重要な人物」にファンズワースが選ばれた。ファンズワースが亡くなった後のインタビューで，妻のペムは，ニール・アームストロングの月面着陸が放送されたことを回想した。ファンズワースは，一緒にテレビを見ながらこう言っていた。「ペム，これですべてが報われた」彼の物語は，十代の夢と高校時代の黒板の絵に常に結びつけられている。空中に動画を送るという夢，そして，その黒板に描いた絵。

MET 2022 本 (2) 解答

解答付き英文を見ながら，英語の音声をもう一度聞いてみよう。

In the following years, he further improved the system so (**that**)[1] it could successfully broadcast live images. The US government gave him (**a**)[2] patent for this system in 1930. However, Farnsworth was not (**the**)[3] only one working on such a system. A giant company, RCA (Radio Corporation of America), (**also**)[4] saw a bright future for television and did (**not**)[5] want to miss the opportunity. They recruited Vladimir Zworykin, (**who**)[6] had already worked on an electronic television system and had earned (**a**)[7] patent as early as 1923. Yet, in 1931, they offered Farnsworth (**a**)[8] large sum of money to sell them (**his**)[9] patent as his system was superior to that (**of**)[10] Zworykin's. He refused this offer, which started a patent war between Farnsworth and RCA. (**The**)[11] company took legal action against Farnsworth, claiming that Zworykin's 1923 patent had priority even though he (**had**)[12] never made a working version of his system. Farnsworth lost (**the**)[13] first two rounds of the court case. However, in the final round, (**the**)[14] teacher who had copied Farnsworth's blackboard drawings gave evidence that Farnsworth did (**have**)[15] the idea of an electronic television system at least (**a**)[16] year before Zworykin's patent was issued. In 1934, a judge approved Farnsworth's patent claim on (**the**)[17] strength of handwritten notes made by his old (**high**)[18] school teacher, Tolman. Farnsworth died in 1971 at the age (**of**)[19] 64. He held about 300 US and foreign patents, mostly in radio and television, (**and**)[20] in 1999, TIME magazine included Farnsworth in Time 100: The Most Important People of the Century. In an interview after his death, Farnsworth's (**wife**)[21] Pem recalled Neil Armstrong's moon landing being broadcast. Watching the television with her, Farnsworth had (**said**)[22], "Pem, this has made it all worthwhile." (**His**)[23] story will always be tied to his teenage dream (**of**)[24] sending moving pictures through the air and those blackboard drawings at his (**high**)[25] school.

英語の音声を聞きながら，（　　）の中に，英単語を入れてください。

When asked "Are you a morning person?" some reply "No, I'm (　　　　)[1] night owl." Such people can concentrate and create at night. (　　　　)[2] the other end of the clock, a well-known proverb claims: "(　　　　)[3] early bird catches the worm," which means that waking early is (　　　　)[4] way to get food, win prizes, (　　　　)[5] reach goals. The lark is a morning singer, so early birds, (　　　　)[6] opposite of owls, are larks. Creatures active during the day (　　　　)[7] "diurnal" and those emerging at night are "nocturnal." Yet another proverb states: "Early to (　　　　)[8], early to rise makes a man healthy, wealthy, and (　　　　)[9]." Larks may jump out of bed (　　　　)[10] welcome the morning with a big breakfast, while owls (　　　　)[11] the snooze button, getting ready at the last minute, usually without breakfast. They (　　　　)[12] have fewer meals, but they eat late (　　　　)[13] the day. Not exercising after meals can cause weight gain. Perhaps larks (　　　　)[14] healthier. Owls must work or learn on (　　　　)[15] lark schedule. Most schooling occurs before 4:00 p.m., so young larks may perform certain tasks better. Business deals made early (　　　　)[16] the day may make some larks wealthier. (　　　　)[17] makes one person a lark and another an owl? One theory suggests preference (　　　　)[18] day or night has to do (　　　　)[19] time of birth. In 2010, Cleveland State University researchers found evidence that not (　　　　)[20] does a person's internal clock start at the moment of birth, (　　　　)[21] that those born at night might have lifelong challenges performing during daytime hours. Usually, their world experience begins with darkness. Since traditional study (   )^{22} and office work happen in daylight, we assume that (   )^{23} begins in the morning. People asleep are not first in (   )^{24}, and might miss chances. Does everyone follow the system of beginning (   )^{25} in the morning? The Jewish people, an approximately 6,000-year-old religious group, believe a (   )^{26} is measured from sundown until the following sundown—from eve (   )^{27} eve. Christians continue this tradition with Christmas Eve.

MET 2022 本（3）日本語訳

問題英文の日本語訳を確認しよう。

「あなたは朝型ですか？」と尋ねると，「いいえ，夜型です」と答える人もいる。そういう人は夜に集中して創作することができる。時計の反対側には，「早起きは三文の徳」という有名なことわざがある。これは，早起きは，食べ物を手に入れ，賞品を獲得し，目標を達成する方法であることを意味する。ヒバリは，朝，歌う鳥なので，早起きの鳥は，フクロウとは反対のヒバリだ。日中に活動する生き物は「昼行性」，夜に活動する生き物は「夜行性」と言う。さらに別のことわざに，「早寝早起きは，人を健康にし，裕福にし，賢くする」というものがある。ヒバリは寝床から飛び起きて，朝食をたっぷり目の前にして，朝を迎えられるが，フクロウは，目覚まし時計を押して，最後の最後で，やっと準備ができる。だいたい，直朝食は抜きで。フクロウは，食事の量が少ないかもしれないが，日中，遅く食事をする。食後に運動をしないと体重増加の原因になる。おそらくヒバリの方が健康的だと言える。フクロウは，ヒバリのようなスケジュールに合わせて，仕事をしたり学習したりしなければならない。ほとんどの学校教育は，午後4時前までに行われるので，若いヒバリは，特定の作業をより効率よく実行できる可能性がある。午前中に取引が行われれば，より裕福になるヒバリもいることになる。なぜ，ある人はヒバリであり，ある人はフクロウであるのだろうか？　一説によると，昼間や夜間を好むのは，出生時間と関係があるという。2010年，クリーブランド州立大学の研究者らは，次のような証拠を発見した。人間の体内時計は，出生の瞬間に始まるだけでなく，夜に生まれた人は，生涯を通じて昼間の活動に問題を抱えている可能性があるということへの証拠だ。通常，彼らの世界体験は暗闇から始まる。従来の勉強時間や事務作業が日中であるため，1日は，午前中に始まると想定されている。眠っている人は列の先頭におらず，チャンスを逃す可能性がある。誰もが，朝に一日が始まるというシステムに従っているのだろうか？　ユダヤ人は，約6,000年の歴史を持つ宗教集団であるが，こう信じている。1日は日没から次の日没までであると。つまりイブからイブまでであると。キリスト教徒は，クリスマスイブとともに，この伝統を守っている。

MET 2022 本 (3) 解答

解答付き英文を見ながら，英語の音声をもう一度聞いてみよう。

When asked "Are you a morning person?" some reply "No, I'm (**a**)[1] night owl." Such people can concentrate and create at night. (**At**)[2] the other end of the clock, a well-known proverb claims: "(**The**)[3] early bird catches the worm," which means that waking early is (**the**)[4] way to get food, win prizes, (**and**)[5] reach goals. The lark is a morning singer, so early birds, (**the**)[6] opposite of owls, are larks. Creatures active during the day (**are**)[7] "diurnal" and those emerging at night are "nocturnal." Yet another proverb states: "Early to (**bed**)[8], early to rise makes a man healthy, wealthy, and (**wise**)[9]." Larks may jump out of bed (**and**)[10] welcome the morning with a big breakfast, while owls (**hit**)[11] the snooze button, getting ready at the last minute, usually without breakfast. They (**may**)[12] have fewer meals, but they eat late (**in**)[13] the day. Not exercising after meals can cause weight gain. Perhaps larks (**are**)[14] healthier. Owls must work or learn on (**the**)[15] lark schedule. Most schooling occurs before 4:00 p.m., so young larks may perform certain tasks better. Business deals made early (**in**)[16] the day may make some larks wealthier. (**What**)[17] makes one person a lark and another an owl? One theory suggests preference (**for**)[18] day or night has to do (**with**)[19] time of birth. In 2010, Cleveland State University researchers found evidence that not (**only**)[20] does a person's internal clock start at the moment of birth, (**but**)[21] that those born at night might have lifelong challenges performing during daytime hours. Usually, their world experience begins with darkness. Since traditional study (**time**)[22] and office work happen in daylight, we assume that (**day**)[23] begins in the morning. People asleep are not first in (**line**)[24], and might miss chances. Does everyone follow the system of beginning (**days**)[25] in the morning? The Jewish people, an approximately 6,000-year-old religious group, believe a (**day**)[26] is measured from sundown until the following sundown—from eve (**to**)[27] eve. Christians continue this tradition with Christmas Eve.

英語の音声を聞きながら，（　　）の中に，英単語を入れてください。

The Chinese use their system of 12 animals not only (　　)[1] mark years, but to separate each two-hour period of (　　)[2] day. The hour of the (　　)[3], the first period, is from 11:00 p.m. to 1:00 a.m. Chinese culture also begins (　　)[4] day at night. In other words, ancient customs support how owls (　　)[5] time. Research indicates owls are smarter and more creative. (　　)[6], perhaps larks are not always wiser! That is to (　　)[7], larks win "healthy" and sometimes "wealthy," but they may (　　)[8] "wise." In an early report, Richard D. Roberts and Patrick C. Kyllonen state that (　　)[9] tend to be more intelligent. A later, comprehensive study (　　)[10] Franzis Preckel, for which Roberts was one of the co-authors, came (　　)[11] the same conclusion. It is not (　　)[12] good news for owls, though. Not (　　)[13] can schoolwork be a challenge, but they (　　)[14] miss daytime career opportunities and are more likely to enjoy (　　)[15] bad habits of "nightlife," playing at night while larks sleep. Nightlife tends to be expensive. (　　)[16] University of Barcelona study suggests larks are precise, seek perfection, and feel little stress. Owls (　　)[17] new adventures and exciting leisure activities, yet they often have trouble relaxing. (　　)[18] people change? While the results are not all in, studies (　　)[19] young adults seem to say no, we (　　)[20] hard-wired. So, as young people grow and acquire more freedom, (　　)[21] end up returning to their lark or (　　)[22] nature. However, concerns arise that this categorization may not fit everyone. (　　)[23] addition to time of birth possibly being an indication, a report published (　　　　)²⁴ *Nature Communications* suggests that DNA may also affect our habits concerning time. Other works focus (　　　　)²⁵ changes occurring in some people due to aging or illness. (　　　　)²⁶ research in this area appears all the (　　　　)²⁷. A study of university students in Russia suggests that there are six types, (　　　　)²⁸ owls and larks may not be (　　　　)²⁹ only birds around!

43

MET 2022 本 (4) 日本語訳

問題英文の日本語訳を確認しよう。

中国人は，12 匹の動物の体系を使用して，年を決めるだけでなく，一日を 2 時間ごとに区切っている。鼠の刻は，最初の時間で，午後 11 時から午前 1 時までだ。中国の文化もまた，一日を夜から始めている。言い換えれば，古代の習慣は，フクロウの時間の見方を裏付けているということだ。研究によると，実は，フクロウは，考えられているより賢く，創造的である。したがって，ヒバリが必ずしも賢いというわけではない。つまり，ヒバリは「健康」に勝ち，時には「裕福」になれるが，「賢く」負けることもあるということだ。初期の報告で，リチャード・D・ロバーツとパトリック・C・カイロネンは，こう述べている。フクロウは，考えられているより賢い傾向がある。後になって，フランツィス・プレッケルによる包括的な研究でも，同じ結論が得られた。ロバーツもその共著者の一人である。ただし，フクロウにとっては，いいことばかりではない。フクロウにとって，学業は，困難であるだけでなく，昼間の仕事の機会を逃す可能性があり，「夜遊び」の悪い習慣を楽しみがちになる。ヒバリが眠っている間に夜に遊ぶという習慣だ。ナイトライフは値が張る傾向がある。バルセロナ大学の研究によると，ヒバリは几帳面で，完璧を求め，ストレスをほとんど感じないという。フクロウは，新しい冒険やエキサイティングな遊びを求めているが，リラックスすることがなかなか難しい。人は変われるのだろうか？ 結果が全て揃っているわけではないが，若者を対象とした研究では，そうではないようだ。人は，生まれつき変われないようになっているのだ。そのため，若者が成長してより自由を獲得すると，結局は，ヒバリやフクロウの性質に戻ってしまうのだ。しかしながら，この分類がすべての人に当てはまるわけではないとも言える。出生時間が一定の示唆を与えていることに加えて，Nature Communications に掲載された報告書では，次のことが示唆されている。DNA もまた，時間に関する私たちの習慣に影響を与えている可能性があると。老化や病気によって一部の人々に起こる変化に焦点を当てた研究もある。この分野における新しい研究は，常に発表されている。ロシアの大学生を対象とした研究では，次のことが示唆されている。鳥は，実は，6 種類存在し，したがって，フクロウとヒバリだけが，周りに存在する鳥ではないということだ。

MET 2022 本 (4) 解答

解答付き英文を見ながら，英語の音声をもう一度聞いてみよう。

The Chinese use their system of 12 animals not only (**to**)[1] mark years, but to separate each two-hour period of (**the**)[2] day. The hour of the (**rat**)[3], the first period, is from 11:00 p.m. to 1:00 a.m. Chinese culture also begins (**the**)[4] day at night. In other words, ancient customs support how owls (**view**)[5] time. Research indicates owls are smarter and more creative. (**So**)[6], perhaps larks are not always wiser! That is to (**say**)[7], larks win "healthy" and sometimes "wealthy," but they may (**lose**)[8] "wise." In an early report, Richard D. Roberts and Patrick C. Kyllonen state that (**owls**)[9] tend to be more intelligent. A later, comprehensive study (**by**)[10] Franzis Preckel, for which Roberts was one of the co-authors, came (**to**)[11] the same conclusion. It is not (**all**)[12] good news for owls, though. Not (**only**)[13] can schoolwork be a challenge, but they (**may**)[14] miss daytime career opportunities and are more likely to enjoy (**the**)[15] bad habits of "nightlife," playing at night while larks sleep. Nightlife tends to be expensive. (**A**)[16] University of Barcelona study suggests larks are precise, seek perfection, and feel little stress. Owls (**seek**)[17] new adventures and exciting leisure activities, yet they often have trouble relaxing. (**Can**)[18] people change? While the results are not all in, studies (**of**)[19] young adults seem to say no, we (**are**)[20] hardwired. So, as young people grow and acquire more freedom, (**they**)[21] end up returning to their lark or (**owl**)[22] nature. However, concerns arise that this categorization may not fit everyone. (**In**)[23] addition to time of birth possibly being an indication, a report published (**in**)[24] *Nature Communications* suggests that DNA may also affect our habits concerning time. Other works focus (**on**)[25] changes occurring in some people due to aging or illness. (**New**)[26] research in this area appears all the (**time**)[27]. A study of university students in Russia suggests that there are six types, (**so**)[28] owls and larks may not be (**the**)[29] only birds around!

英語の音声を聞きながら，（　）の中に，英単語を入れてください。

The world is full of various types of plastic. (　　　)[1] around, and you will see dozens of plastic items. (　　　)[2] closer and you will notice a recycling symbol on (　　　)[3]. In Japan, you might have seen the first symbol (　　　)[4] Figure 1 below, but the United States and Europe have a (　　　)[5] detailed classification. These recycling symbols look like a triangle of chasing pointers, or sometimes (　　　)[6] simple triangle with a number from one to seven inside. This system (　　　)[7] started in 1988 by the Society of the Plastics Industry (　　　)[8] the US, but since 2008 it has been administered (　　　)[9] an international standards organization, ASTM (American Society for Testing and Materials) International. Recycling symbols provide important data about the chemical composition of plastic used (　　　)[10] its recyclability. However, a plastic recycling symbol on an object does (　　　)[11] always mean that the item can (　　　)[12] recycled. It only shows what type of plastic (　　　)[13] is made from and that (　　　)[14] might be recyclable. So, what do these numbers mean? One group (　　　)[15] considered to be safe for the human (　　　)[16], while the other group could be problematic in certain circumstances. Let us (　　　)[17] at the safer group first. High-density Polyethylene is a recycle-type 2 plastic and (　　　)[18] commonly called HDPE. It is non-toxic and can be (　　　)[19] in the human body for heart valves and artificial joints. (　　　)[20] is strong and can be used (　　　)[21] temperatures as low as $-40℃$ and as (　　　)[22] as $100℃$. HDPE can be reused without any harm (　　　)[23] is also suitable for beer-bottle cases, milk jugs, chairs, (   )^{24} toys. Type 2 products can be recycled several times. Type 4 products are made (   )^{25} Low-density Polyethylene (LDPE). They are safe to use (   )^{26} are flexible. LDPE is used for squeezable bottles, and bread wrapping. Currently, (   )^{27} little Type 4 plastic is recycled.

MET 2022 本（5）日本語訳

問題英文の日本語訳を確認しよう。

世界は，さまざまな種類のプラスチックで溢れている。周りを見回すと，何十ものプラスチック製品が見える。よく見ると，リサイクルマークが付いていることに気づくことがある。日本では，以下の図 1 の最初の記号を目にしたことがあるかもしれないが，米国と欧州ではより詳細な分類がある。これらのリサイクル記号は，矢印が追いかけている三角形のように見えたり，中には 1 から 7 までの数字が入った単純な三角形のように見える。この制度は 1988 年に米国プラスチック産業協会によって開始されたが，2008 年からは国際標準化団体，国際 ASTM（American Society for Testing and Materials）によって管理されている。リサイクル記号は，重要なデータを提供してくれる。使用されるプラスチックの化学組成とそのリサイクル可能性に関して。ただし，物品にプラスチックリサイクルマークが付いていても，必ずしもその物品がリサイクル可能であることを意味するわけではない。どのような種類のプラスチックで作られているか，そしてリサイクル可能かどうかだけが示されている。では，これらの数字は何を意味するのか？ 1 つのグループは，人体にとって安全であると考えられているが，もう 1 つのグループは，特定の状況では問題となる可能性がある。まず安全なグループを見てみよう。高密度ポリエチレンは，リサイクルタイプ 2 のプラスチックで，一般に HDPE と呼ばれる。毒性はなく，人体でも使用できる。心臓弁や人工関節などに。強度があり，下は −40℃ から，上は 100℃ まで使用できる。HDPE は無害に再利用でき，ビール瓶のケース，ミルク入れ，椅子，おもちゃなどにも適している。タイプ 2 製品は，数回リサイクルできる。タイプ 4 製品は低密度ポリエチレン（LDPE）から作られている。安全に使用でき，柔軟性もある。LDPE は，ぎゅっと押せる飲み物の入れ物やパンの包装などに使用されている。現在，タイプ 4 プラスチックは，ほとんどリサイクルされていない。

MET 2022 本 (5) 解答

解答付き英文を見ながら，英語の音声をもう一度聞いてみよう。

The world is full of various types of plastic. (**Look**)[1] around, and you will see dozens of plastic items. (**Look**)[2] closer and you will notice a recycling symbol on (**them**)[3]. In Japan, you might have seen the first symbol (**in**)[4] Figure 1 below, but the United States and Europe have a (**more**)[5] detailed classification. These recycling symbols look like a triangle of chasing pointers, or sometimes (**a**)[6] simple triangle with a number from one to seven inside. This system (**was**)[7] started in 1988 by the Society of the Plastics Industry (**in**)[8] the US, but since 2008 it has been administered (**by**)[9] an international standards organization, ASTM (American Society for Testing and Materials) International. Recycling symbols provide important data about the chemical composition of plastic used (**and**)[10] its recyclability. However, a plastic recycling symbol on an object does (**not**)[11] always mean that the item can (**be**)[12] recycled. It only shows what type of plastic (**it**)[13] is made from and that (**it**)[14] might be recyclable. So, what do these numbers mean? One group (**is**)[15] considered to be safe for the human (**body**)[16], while the other group could be problematic in certain circumstances. Let us (**look**)[17] at the safer group first. High-density Polyethylene is a recycle-type 2 plastic and (**is**)[18] commonly called HDPE. It is non-toxic and can be (**used**)[19] in the human body for heart valves and artificial joints. (**It**)[20] is strong and can be used (**at**)[21] temperatures as low as $-40°C$ and as (**high**)[22] as $100°C$. HDPE can be reused without any harm (**and**)[23] is also suitable for beer-bottle cases, milk jugs, chairs, (**and**)[24] toys. Type 2 products can be recycled several times. Type 4 products are made (**from**)[25] Low-density Polyethylene (LDPE). They are safe to use (**and**)[26] are flexible. LDPE is used for squeezable bottles, and bread wrapping. Currently, (**very**)[27] little Type 4 plastic is recycled.

英語の音声を聞きながら，（　　）の中に，英単語を入れてください。

Polypropylene (PP), a Type 5 material, is the second-most widely produced plastic in the world. (　　　　)[1] is light, non-stretching, and has a high resistance (　　　　)[2] impact, heat, and freezing. It is suitable for furniture, (　　　　)[3] containers, and polymer banknotes such as the Australian dollar. Only 3% (　　　　)[4] Type 5 is recycled. Now let us look (　　　　)[5] the second group, Types 1, 3, 6, and 7. These are more challenging because of (　　　　)[6] chemicals they contain or the difficulty in recycling them. Recycle-type 1 plastic (　　　　)[7] commonly known as PETE (Polyethylene Terephthalate), and is used mainly in (　　　　)[8] and beverage containers. PETE containers—or PET as it is often written (　　　　)[9] Japan—should only be used once as (　　　　)[10] are difficult to clean thoroughly. Also, they should not (　　　　)[11] heated above 70℃ as this can cause some containers to soften (　　　　)[12] change shape. Uncontaminated PETE is easy to recycle and can (　　　　)[13] made into new containers, clothes, or carpets, but (　　　　)[14] PETE is contaminated with Polyvinyl Chloride (PVC), it can make (　　　　)[15] unrecyclable. PVC, Type 3, is thought to be one of the least recyclable plastics known. (　　　　)[16] should only be disposed of by professionals and never (　　　　)[17] fire to at home or (　　　　)[18] the garden. Type 3 plastic is found in shower curtains, pipes, and flooring. Type 6, Polystyrene (PS) or Styrofoam (　　　　)[19] it is often called, is hard to recycle (　　　　)[20] catches fire easily. However, it is cheap to produce and lightweight. (　　　　)[21] is used for disposable drinking cups, instant noodle containers, and other

(   )^{22} packaging. Type 7 plastics (acrylics, nylons, and polycarbonates) are difficult to recycle. Type 7 plastics are often used (   )^{23} the manufacture of vehicle parts such as seats, dashboards, and bumpers. Currently, (   )^{24} about 20% of plastic is recycled, and approximately 55% ends up (   )^{25} a landfill. Therefore, knowledge about different types of plastic could help reduce waste and contribute to (   )^{26} increased awareness of the environment.

MET 2022 本（6）日本語訳

問題英文の日本語訳を確認しよう。

ポリプロピレン（PP）は，タイプ5の材料であるが，世界で2番目に多く生産されているプラスチックだ。軽くて伸びがなく，耐衝撃性，耐熱性，耐寒性にも優れている。家具，食品容器，合成樹脂を含むポリマー紙幣などに適している。ポリマー紙幣は，オーストラリアドルなどに使用されているものだ。タイプ5のうちリサイクルされるのはわずか3%だ。次に，2番目のグループを見てみよう。タイプ1，3，6，および，7だ。これらは，これまで見てきたものより，困難だ。というのも，化学物質が含まれているか，リサイクルが難しいからだ。リサイクルタイプ1のプラスチックは，通称PETE（ポリエチレンテレフタレート）と呼ばれ，主に食品や飲料の容器に使用されている。PETE容器，日本ではPETと呼ばれることが多いが，1回しか使用できない。完全に洗浄するのが難しいからだ。また，70℃以上に加熱してはいけない。加熱すれば，容器が軟化して変形する場合があるからだ。汚染されていないPETEは，リサイクルが簡単で，新しい容器，衣類，カーペットなどに作り変えることができる。しかし，PETEが，ポリ塩化ビニル（PVC）で汚染されている場合，リサイクルできなくなる可能性がある。PVCは，タイプ3であるが，知られているプラスチックの中で最もリサイクルしにくいものの1つであると考えられている。専門家のみが処分するもので，自宅や庭で絶対に火をつけてはいけない。タイプ3プラスチックは，シャワーカーテン，パイプ，床材に使用されている。タイプ6のものには，ポリスチレン（PS），または発泡スチロールとよく呼ばれるものが入るが，リサイクルが難しく，簡単に発火する。ただし，製造コストが安く，軽量だ。使い捨てカップ，インスタントラーメンの容器，他の食品包装に使用されている。タイプ7プラスチック（アクリル，ナイロン，ポリカーボネート）は，リサイクルが困難だ。タイプ7プラスチックは，自動車部品の製造によく使用されている。シート，ダッシュボード，バンパーなどだ。現在，プラスチックの約20%しかリサイクルされておらず，約55%が最終的に埋め立てられている。したがって，さまざまな種類のプラスチックに関する知識は，廃棄物の削減に役立ち，環境意識の向上に貢献する可能性がある。

MET 2022 本 (6) 解答

解答付き英文を見ながら，英語の音声をもう一度聞いてみよう。

Polypropylene (PP), a Type 5 material, is the second-most widely produced plastic in the world. (**It**)[1] is light, non-stretching, and has a high resistance (**to**)[2] impact, heat, and freezing. It is suitable for furniture, (**food**)[3] containers, and polymer banknotes such as the Australian dollar. Only 3% (**of**)[4] Type 5 is recycled. Now let us look (**at**)[5] the second group, Types 1, 3, 6, and 7. These are more challenging because of (**the**)[6] chemicals they contain or the difficulty in recycling them. Recycle-type 1 plastic (**is**)[7] commonly known as PETE (Polyethylene Terephthalate), and is used mainly in (**food**)[8] and beverage containers. PETE containers—or PET as it is often written (**in**)[9] Japan—should only be used once as (**they**)[10] are difficult to clean thoroughly. Also, they should not (**be**)[11] heated above 70℃ as this can cause some containers to soften (**and**)[12] change shape. Uncontaminated PETE is easy to recycle and can (**be**)[13] made into new containers, clothes, or carpets, but (**if**)[14] PETE is contaminated with Polyvinyl Chloride (PVC), it can make (**it**)[15] unrecyclable. PVC, Type 3, is thought to be one of the least recyclable plastics known. (**It**)[16] should only be disposed of by professionals and never (**set**)[17] fire to at home or (**in**)[18] the garden. Type 3 plastic is found in shower curtains, pipes, and flooring. Type 6, Polystyrene (PS) or Styrofoam (**as**)[19] it is often called, is hard to recycle (**and**)[20] catches fire easily. However, it is cheap to produce and lightweight. (**It**)[21] is used for disposable drinking cups, instant noodle containers, and other (**food**)[22] packaging. Type 7 plastics (acrylics, nylons, and polycarbonates) are difficult to recycle. Type 7 plastics are often used (**in**)[23] the manufacture of vehicle parts such as seats, dashboards, and bumpers. Currently, (**only**)[24] about 20% of plastic is recycled, and approximately 55% ends up (**in**)[25] a landfill. Therefore, knowledge about different types of plastic could help reduce waste and contribute to (**an**)[26] increased awareness of the environment.

MET 2023 本 (1)

英語の音声を聞きながら，（　　）の中に，英単語を入れてください。

The ball flew at lightning speed (　　　　)[1] my backhand. It was completely unexpected and (　　　　)[2] had no time to react. (　　　　)[3] lost the point and the match. Defeat... Again! (　　　　)[4] is how it was (　　　　)[5] the first few months when I started playing table tennis. (　　　　)[6] was frustrating, but I now (　　　　)[7] that the sport taught me more (　　　　)[8] simply how to be a better athlete. (　　　　)[9] middle school, I loved football. I was one of (　　　　)[10] top scorers, but I didn't get along (　　　　)[11] my teammates. The coach often said that (　　　　)[12] should be more of a (　　　　)[13] player. I knew I should work (　　　　)[14] the problem, but communication was just (　　　　)[15] my strong point. I had to leave (　　　　)[16] football club when my family moved to (　　　　)[17] new town. I wasn't upset as (　　　　)[18] had decided to stop playing football anyway. My (　　　　)[19] school had a table tennis club, coached by (　　　　)[20] PE teacher, Mr Trent, and I joined that. To (　　　　)[21] honest, I chose table tennis because I thought it would be easier (　　　　)[22] me to play individually. At first, (　　　　)[23] lost more games than I (　　　　)[24]. I was frustrated and often went straight (　　　　)[25] after practice, not speaking to anyone. One day, however, Mr Trent said (　　　　)[26] me, "You could be a (　　　　)[27] player, Ben, but you need to think (　　　　)[28] about your game. What do (　　　　)[29] think you need to do?" "(　　　　)[30] don't know," I replied, "focus on the ball (　　　　)[31]?" "Yes," Mr Trent continued, "but you also need (　　　　)[32] study your opponent's moves and adjust your play accordingly.

Remember, (　　　)³³ opponent is a person, not a (　　　)³⁴." This made a deep impression (　　　)³⁵ me. I deliberately modified my style of (　　　)³⁶, paying closer attention to my opponent's moves. It was (　　　)³⁷ easy, and took a (　　　)³⁸ of concentration. My efforts paid off, however, (　　　)³⁹ my play improved. My confidence grew (　　　)⁴⁰ I started staying behind more after practice.

MET 2023 本（1）日本語訳

問題英文の日本語訳を確認しよう。

ボールは，電光石火のスピードで私のバックハンドに飛んできた。まったく予想外だったので，反応する暇もなかった。点を失い，試合も負けてしまった。敗北，再び！ 私が卓球を始めた最初の数ヶ月はこんな感じだった。悔しい思いをしたが，今ではわかっている。このスポーツを通して，単にいいアスリートになることだけを学んだんじゃないということを。中学時代はサッカーが大好きだった。私は得点王の一人だったが，チームメイトとはうまくいかなかった。コーチにはよく言われた。もっとチームのために動けと。この問題に取り組む必要があることはわかっていたが，コミュニケーションが苦手だった。私は，サッカーを辞めなければならなかった。家族が新しい町に引っ越した時に。別に動揺はしなかった。サッカーをやめると決めていたので。新しい学校には卓球クラブがあって，体育教師のトレント先生が指導していた。私はそこに入部した。正直に言うと，卓球を選んだのは，個人でプレーしやすいと思ったからだ。初めは，勝った試合よりも負けた試合の方が多かった。イライラして，練習後，まっすぐ家に帰ることがよくあった。誰とも話さずに。しかし，ある日，トレント先生は私にこう言った。「ベン，君はいいプレイヤーかもしれないが，自分のゲームについてもっと考える必要がある。何をする必要があると思う？」「わかりません」私は答えた。「もっとボールに集中するってことですか？」「そう」トレント先生は続けた。「でも，対戦相手の動きを研究し，それに応じて自分のプレーを調整する必要もある。いいかい，君の相手は人間なんだってことを忘れちゃだめだよ。ボールじゃなくって」これは心に響いた。私は意図的に自分のプレースタイルを修正し，相手の動きに細心の注意を払うようにした。簡単ではなかった。集中力が必要だった。しかし，私の努力は報われ，私のプレーは向上した。自信がつき，練習後も，居残り練習することが多くなった。

MET 2023 本（1）解答

解答付き英文を見ながら，英語の音声をもう一度聞いてみよう。

The ball flew at lightning speed (**to**)^1 my backhand. It was completely unexpected and (**I**)^2 had no time to react. (**I**)^3 lost the point and the match. Defeat... Again! (**This**)^4 is how it was (**in**)^5 the first few months when I started playing table tennis. (**It**)^6 was frustrating, but I now (**know**)^7 that the sport taught me more (**than**)^8 simply how to be a better athlete. (**In**)^9 middle school, I loved football. I was one of (**the**)^{10} top scorers, but I didn't get along (**with**)^{11} my teammates. The coach often said that (**I**)^{12} should be more of a (**team**)^{13} player. I knew I should work (**on**)^{14} the problem, but communication was just (**not**)^{15} my strong point. I had to leave (**the**)^{16} football club when my family moved to (**a**)^{17} new town. I wasn't upset as (**I**)^{18} had decided to stop playing football anyway. My (**new**)^{19} school had a table tennis club, coached by (**the**)^{20} PE teacher, Mr Trent, and I joined that. To (**be**)^{21} honest, I chose table tennis because I thought it would be easier (**for**)^{22} me to play individually. At first, (**I**)^{23} lost more games than I (**won**)^{24}. I was frustrated and often went straight (**home**)^{25} after practice, not speaking to anyone. One day, however, Mr Trent said (**to**)^{26} me, "You could be a (**good**)^{27} player, Ben, but you need to think (**more**)^{28} about your game. What do (**you**)^{29} think you need to do?" "(**I**)^{30} don't know," I replied, "focus on the ball (**more**)^{31}?" "Yes," Mr Trent continued, "but you also need (**to**)^{32} study your opponent's moves and adjust your play accordingly. Remember, (**your**)^{33} opponent is a person, not a (**ball**)^{34}." This made a deep impression (**on**)^{35} me. I deliberately modified my style of (**play**)^{36}, paying closer attention to my opponent's moves. It was (**not**)^{37} easy, and took a (**lot**)^{38} of concentration. My efforts paid off, however, (**and**)^{39} my play improved. My confidence grew (**and**)^{40} I started staying behind more after practice.

MET 2023 本（2）

英語の音声を聞きながら，（　　）の中に，英単語を入れてください。

I was turning into a (　　　　)[1] player and my classmates tried to talk (　　　　)[2] me more than before. I thought (　　　　)[3] I was becoming popular, but our conversations seemed (　　　　)[4] end before they really got started. Although my (　　　　)[5] might have improved, my communication skills obviously hadn't. My older brother Patrick was one (　　　　)[6] the few people I could communicate with (　　　　)[7]. One day, I tried to explain my problems (　　　　)[8] communication to him, but couldn't make (　　　　)[9] understand. We switched to talking about table tennis. "What do (　　　　)[10] actually enjoy about it?" he asked me curiously. I (　　　　)[11] I loved analysing my opponent's movements and making instant decisions about the (　　　　)[12] move. Patrick looked thoughtful. "That sounds like the (　　　　)[13] of skill we use when (　　　　)[14] communicate," he said. At that (　　　　)[15], I didn't understand, but soon after our conversation, (　　　　)[16] won a silver medal in a table tennis tournament. (　　　　)[17] classmates seemed really pleased. One of them, George, came running over. " Hey, Ben!" (　　　　)[18] said, "Let's have a party to celebrate!" Without thinking, (　　　　)[19] replied, "I can't. I've got practice." He looked a (　　　　)[20] hurt and walked off without saying anything else. (　　　　)[21] was he upset? I thought about this incident (　　　　)[22] a long time. Why (　　　　)[23] he suggest a party? Should I have (　　　　)[24] something different? A lot of questions came (　　　　)[25] my mind, but then (　　　　)[26] realised that he was just being (　　　　)[27]. If I'd said, "Great idea. Thank you! (　　　　)[28] me talk to Mr Trent and (   )^{29} if I can get (   )^{30} time off practice," then maybe the outcome would (   )^{31} been better. At that moment Patrick's words made sense. Without attempting (   )^{32} grasp someone's intention, I wouldn't know how to respond. I'm still (   )^{33} the best communicator in the world, (   )^{34} I definitely feel more confident in (   )^{35} communication skills now than before. Next year, (   )^{36} friends and I are going to co-ordinate (   )^{37} table tennis league with other schools.

MET 2023 本 (2) 日本語訳

問題英文の日本語訳を確認しよう。

私はスター選手になりつつあり，クラスメートは以前よりも私に話しかけようとしてきた。人気が出てきたと思ったが，クラスメートとの会話は，始まる前に終わってしまった。私のプレーは向上したかもしれなかったが，明らかに，コミュニケーション能力は向上していなかった。兄のパトリックは，私とうまくコミュニケーションが取れる数少ない一人だった。ある日，私は，兄にコミュニケーションの問題を説明しようとした。が，兄に理解してもらうことができなかった。話題は卓球の話に移った。「実際，卓球をやってて，何が楽しいの？」兄は興味深そうに尋ねてきた。私はこう言った。相手の動きを分析し，次の動きについて瞬時に判断するのが大好きなんだ。パトリックは，何かを考えているようだった。そして，こう言った。「それは，コミュニケーションをとる時に使うスキルのような気がする」その時は理解できなかったが，会話の後すぐ，卓球の大会で銀メダルを獲得した。クラスメートは本当に喜んでいたように見えた。そのうちの一人，ジョージが駆け寄ってきた。「おい，ベン！」ジョージはこう言った。「お祝いのパーティーをしないか！」私は何も考えずに，こう答えてしまった。「いや，いいよ。だって，練習があるから」ジョージは少し傷ついたように見えたが，何も言わずに立ち去った。なぜジョージは動揺したんだろう？ 私はこの件についてしばらく考えてみた。なぜジョージはパーティーをやろうなんて言ったんだろう？ 私は，何か違うことを言うべきだったのかな？ 次から次に疑問が頭に浮かんだが，私は気付いた。ジョージはただ親切だっただけなんじゃないか。もし私がこう言っていたら，「素晴らしい。ありがとう！ トレント先生に相談して，練習を少し休めるかどうか聞いてみるよ」そうすれば，もっといい結果になっていたかもしれない。その瞬間，パトリックの言葉が腑に落ちた。相手の意図を汲み取ろうとしなければ，どう答えていいかわからない。私はまだ世界で最高のコミュニケーション能力があるわけではないが，間違いなく，自信を持っている。以前よりも，自分のコミュニケーション能力に。来年，友人と私で，他の学校と卓球リーグをコーディネートするつもりだ。

MET 2023 本 (2) 解答

解答付き英文を見ながら，英語の音声をもう一度聞いてみよう。

I was turning into a (**star**)[1] player and my classmates tried to talk (**to**)[2] me more than before. I thought (**that**)[3] I was becoming popular, but our conversations seemed (**to**)[4] end before they really got started. Although my (**play**)[5] might have improved, my communication skills obviously hadn't. My older brother Patrick was one (**of**)[6] the few people I could communicate with (**well**)[7]. One day, I tried to explain my problems (**with**)[8] communication to him, but couldn't make (**him**)[9] understand. We switched to talking about table tennis. "What do (**you**)[10] actually enjoy about it?" he asked me curiously. I (**said**)[11] I loved analysing my opponent's movements and making instant decisions about the (**next**)[12] move. Patrick looked thoughtful. "That sounds like the (**kind**)[13] of skill we use when (**we**)[14] communicate," he said. At that (**time**)[15], I didn't understand, but soon after our conversation, (**I**)[16] won a silver medal in a table tennis tournament. (**My**)[17] classmates seemed really pleased. One of them, George, came running over. "Hey, Ben!" (**he**)[18] said, "Let's have a party to celebrate!" Without thinking, (**I**)[19] replied, "I can't. I've got practice." He looked a (**bit**)[20] hurt and walked off without saying anything else. (**Why**)[21] was he upset? I thought about this incident (**for**)[22] a long time. Why (**did**)[23] he suggest a party? Should I have (**said**)[24] something different? A lot of questions came (**to**)[25] my mind, but then (**I**)[26] realised that he was just being (**kind**)[27]. If I'd said, "Great idea. Thank you! (**Let**)[28] me talk to Mr Trent and (**see**)[29] if I can get (**some**)[30] time off practice," then maybe the outcome would (**have**)[31] been better. At that moment Patrick's words made sense. Without attempting (**to**)[32] grasp someone's intention, I wouldn't know how to respond. I'm still (**not**)[33] the best communicator in the world, (**but**)[34] I definitely feel more confident in (**my**)[35] communication skills now than before. Next year, (**my**)[36] friends and I are going to co-ordinate (**the**)[37] table tennis league with other schools.

英語の音声を聞きながら，（　　）の中に，英単語を入れてください。

Collecting has existed at all levels of society, across cultures (　　　　)[1] age groups since early times.　Museums are proof that things have (　　　　)[2] collected, saved, and passed down for future generations. There are various reasons (　　　　)[3] starting a collection.　For example, Ms. A enjoys going to yard sales every Saturday morning (　　　　)[4] her children.　At yard sales, people sell unwanted things (　　　　)[5] front of their houses.　One day, while looking for antique dishes, an unusual painting caught (　　　　)[6] eye and she bought it (　　　　)[7] only a few dollars. Over (　　　　)[8], she found similar pieces that left an impression (　　　　)[9] her, and she now (　　　　)[10] a modest, collection of artwork, some of which (　　　　)[11] be worth more than she (　　　　)[12].　One person's trash can be another person's treasure.　Regardless of how someone's collection (　　　　)[13] started, it is human nature to collect things.　In 1988, researchers Brenda Danet (　　　　)[14] Tamar Katriel analyzed 80 years of studies on children under the age (　　　　)[15] 10, and found that about 90% collected something.　This shows us (　　　　)[16] people like to gather things from an early (　　　　)[17].　Even after becoming adults, people continue collecting stuff.　Researchers in the field generally agree that approximately one third (　　　　)[18] adults maintain this behavior.　Why is this? (　　　　)[19] primary explanation is related to emotions.　Some save greeting cards (　　　　)[20] friends and family, dried flowers from special events, seashells from a (　　　　)[21] at the beach, old photos, and (　　　　)[22] on.　For others, their collection is a connection (　　　　)[23]

their youth. They may have baseball cards, comic books, dolls, or miniature (   )^{24} that they have kept since (   )^{25} were small. Others have an attachment to history; (   )^{26} seek and hold onto historical documents, signed letters (   )^{27} autographs from famous people, and so forth. For (   )^{28} individuals there is a social reason. People collect things such as (   )^{29} to share, show, and even trade, making (   )^{30} friends this way.

MET 2023 本（3）日本語訳

問題英文の日本語訳を確認しよう。

収集という趣味は，社会のあらゆるレベルで昔から存在してきた。文化や年齢層を越えて。博物館は，その証拠だ。物が収集され，保存され，後世に引き継がれてきたことの。コレクションを始める理由はさまざまだ。例えば，A さんは毎週土曜日の朝，子供たちと一緒にヤードセールに行くのが楽しみだとしよう。ヤードセールでは，家の前で不要なものが売られる。ある日，アンティークの食器を探していると，珍しい絵が目に留まり，それをわずか数ドルで購入した。時間が経つにつれ，彼女は印象に残った似た作品を見つけ，今ではささやかなアート作品のコレクションを所有している。そして，その中には支払った金額よりも価値があるものもある。ある人のゴミが別の人にとっては宝物になることもある。コレクションを始めたきっかけが何であれ，物を集めるのは人間の本能だ。1988 年，研究者のブレンダ・ダネットとタマー・カトリエルは，10 歳未満の子供に関する 80 年間の研究を分析し，こんなことを発見した。それは，約 90％が何かを収集しているということだ。これは，次のことを示している。人は，幼い頃から物を集めるのが好きだということだ。大人になってからも，人は物を集め続ける。この分野の研究者は，おおむね，次のことに同意している。成人の約 3 分の 1 がこの行動を維持しているということだ。なぜだろう？ 第一の説明は，感情に関連している。友人や家族からのグリーティングカード，特別なイベントのドライフラワー，ビーチで過ごしたあの日の貝殻，古い写真などを保存している人もいる。コレクション自体が青春時代とのつながりである人というもいる。野球カード，漫画本，人形，ミニカーなど，小さい頃からためてきた，そんなものを持っている人がいるかもしれない。歴史に愛着を持っている人もいる。そういう人は，歴史的文書，有名人の署名入りの手紙やサインなどを探し，保持している。社会的な理由がある人もいる。ピンなどを集めて，共有したり，見せたり，交換したりして，こういった方法で新しい友人を作る。

MET 2023 本 (3) 解答

解答付き英文を見ながら，英語の音声をもう一度聞いてみよう。

Collecting has existed at all levels of society, across cultures (**and**)[1] age groups since early times. Museums are proof that things have (**been**)[2] collected, saved, and passed down for future generations. There are various reasons (**for**)[3] starting a collection. For example, Ms. A enjoys going to yard sales every Saturday morning (**with**)[4] her children. At yard sales, people sell unwanted things (**in**)[5] front of their houses. One day, while looking for antique dishes, an unusual painting caught (**her**)[6] eye and she bought it (**for**)[7] only a few dollars. Over (**time**)[8], she found similar pieces that left an impression (**on**)[9] her, and she now (**has**)[10] a modest, collection of artwork, some of which (**may**)[11] be worth more than she (**paid**)[12]. One person's trash can be another person's treasure. Regardless of how someone's collection (**was**)[13] started, it is human nature to collect things. In 1988, researchers Brenda Danet (**and**)[14] Tamar Katriel analyzed 80 years of studies on children under the age (**of**)[15] 10, and found that about 90% collected something. This shows us (**that**)[16] people like to gather things from an early (**age**)[17]. Even after becoming adults, people continue collecting stuff. Researchers in the field generally agree that approximately one third (**of**)[18] adults maintain this behavior. Why is this? (**The**)[19] primary explanation is related to emotions. Some save greeting cards (**from**)[20] friends and family, dried flowers from special events, seashells from a (**day**)[21] at the beach, old photos, and (**so**)[22] on. For others, their collection is a connection (**to**)[23] their youth. They may have baseball cards, comic books, dolls, or miniature (**cars**)[24] that they have kept since (**they**)[25] were small. Others have an attachment to history; (**they**)[26] seek and hold onto historical documents, signed letters (**and**)[27] autographs from famous people, and so forth. For (**some**)[28] individuals there is a social reason. People collect things such as (**pins**)[29] to share, show, and even trade, making (**new**)[30] friends this way.

英語の音声を聞きながら, (　　) の中に, 英単語を入れてください。

Others, like some holders of Guinness World Records, appreciate the (　　　)^1 they achieve for their unique collection. Cards, stickers, stamps, coins, and toys (　　　)^2 topped the "usual" collection list, but some collectors (　　　)^3 toward the more unexpected. In September 2014, Guinness World Records recognized Harry Sperl, of Germany, (　　　)^4 having the largest hamburger-related collection in the world, with 3,724 items; (　　　)^5 T-shirts to pillows to dog toys, Sperl's (　　　)^6 is filled with all things "hamburger." Similarly, Liu Fuchang, of China, (　　　)^7 a collector of playing cards. He has 11,087 different (　　　)^8. Perhaps the easiest motivation to understand is pleasure. Some people start collections (　　　)^9 pure enjoyment. They may purchase and (　　　)^{10} up paintings just to gaze (　　　)^{11} frequently, or they may collect audio recordings and oldfashioned vinyl records (　　　)^{12} enjoy listening to their favorite music. This type of collector (　　　)^{13} unlikely to be very interested in (　　　)^{14} monetary value of their treasured music, while others collect objects specifically as an investment. While it (　　　)^{15} possible to download certain classic games for free, having the (　　　)^{16} game unopened in its original packaging, in "(　　　)^{17} condition," can make the game worth (　　　)^{18} lot. Owning various valuable "collector's items" could ensure some financial security. This behavior of collecting things (　　　)^{19} definitely continue into the distant future. Although the reasons why people (　　　)^{20} things will likely remain the same, advances in technology (　　　)^{21}

have an influence on collections. As technology (   )^{22} remove physical constraints, it is now possible for (   )^{23} individual to have vast digital libraries of music (   )^{24} art that would have been unimaginable 30 years (   )^{25}. It is unclear, though, what other impacts technology will (   )^{26} on collections. Can you even imagine (   )^{27} form and scale that the (   )^{28} generation's collections will take?

MET 2023 本 (4) 日本語訳

問題英文の日本語訳を確認しよう。

一部のギネス世界記録保持者のように、独自のコレクションで得た名声を喜ぶ人もいる。カード、ステッカー、切手、コイン、おもちゃは、「通常の」コレクションリストの上位にランクインしているが、コレクターの中には、予想外のものに興味を持っている人もいる。2014 年 9 月、ギネス世界記録は、ドイツのハリー・シュパールを認定した。3,724 点に及ぶ世界最大のハンバーガー関連コレクションを持つ者として。T シャツから枕、犬のおもちゃに至るまで、シュパールの部屋は「ハンバーガー」で満たされている。同様に、中国の劉福昌も、トランプのコレクターだ。彼は、11,087 も異なるトランプのセットを持っている。おそらく、最も理解しやすい動機は、喜びだ。純粋に楽しむために、コレクションを始める人もいる。絵画を購入して飾って、頻繁に眺めたり、オーディオ録音や昔ながらのビニールレコードを収集して、お気に入りの音楽を聴いたりする人もいる。このタイプのコレクターは、自分の大切な音楽の金銭的価値にあまり興味を持っていない。一方、特に投資のために、物を収集する人もいる。特定の古典的なゲームを無料でダウンロードすることは可能だが、同じゲームを元のパッケージで未開封の「新品の状態」で入手すると、そのゲームに大きな価値が生じる。さまざまな貴重な「コレクターズアイテム」を所有することで、一定の経済的安全を確保できる。この物を集めるという行為は、きっと遠い未来まで続く。人々が物を保管する理由は今後も変わらないと思われるが、テクノロジーの進歩はコレクションにも影響を与えるだろう。テクノロジーが物理的な制約を取り除けるようになったことで、個人が、膨大なデジタル ライブラリーを持つことが可能になった。30 年前には想像もできなかった音楽や芸術の図書館だ。ただし、テクノロジーがコレクションに対して、他のどんな影響を与えるかは不明だ。あなたは、想像できるかな？次世代のコレクションがどのような形式と規模になっているか。

MET 2023 本（4）解答

解答付き英文を見ながら，英語の音声をもう一度聞いてみよう。

Others, like some holders of Guinness World Records, appreciate the (**fame**)[1] they achieve for their unique collection. Cards, stickers, stamps, coins, and toys (**have**)[2] topped the "usual" collection list, but some collectors (**lean**)[3] toward the more unexpected. In September 2014, Guinness World Records recognized Harry Sperl, of Germany, (**for**)[4] having the largest hamburger-related collection in the world, with 3,724 items; (**from**)[5] T-shirts to pillows to dog toys, Sperl's (**room**)[6] is filled with all things "hamburger." Similarly, Liu Fuchang, of China, (**is**)[7] a collector of playing cards. He has 11,087 different (**sets**)[8]. Perhaps the easiest motivation to understand is pleasure. Some people start collections (**for**)[9] pure enjoyment. They may purchase and (**put**)[10] up paintings just to gaze (**at**)[11] frequently, or they may collect audio recordings and oldfashioned vinyl records (**to**)[12] enjoy listening to their favorite music. This type of collector (**is**)[13] unlikely to be very interested in (**the**)[14] monetary value of their treasured music, while others collect objects specifically as an investment. While it (**is**)[15] possible to download certain classic games for free, having the (**same**)[16] game unopened in its original packaging, in "(**mint**)[17] condition," can make the game worth (**a**)[18] lot. Owning various valuable "collector's items" could ensure some financial security. This behavior of collecting things (**will**)[19] definitely continue into the distant future. Although the reasons why people (**keep**)[20] things will likely remain the same, advances in technology (**will**)[21] have an influence on collections. As technology (**can**)[22] remove physical constraints, it is now possible for (**an**)[23] individual to have vast digital libraries of music (**and**)[24] art that would have been unimaginable 30 years (**ago**)[25]. It is unclear, though, what other impacts technology will (**have**)[26] on collections. Can you even imagine (**the**)[27] form and scale that the (**next**)[28] generation's collections will take?

MET 2023 本 (5)

英語の音声を聞きながら，（　　）の中に，英単語を入れてください。

Ask someone to name the world's toughest animal, (　　　　)[1] they might say the Bactrian camel as (　　　　)[2] can survive in temperatures as high (　　　　)[3] 50℃, or the Arctic fox which can survive (　　　　)[4] temperatures lower than −58℃. However, both answers would be wrong as (　　　　)[5] is widely believed that the tardigrade is (　　　　)[6] toughest creature on earth. Tardigrades, also known as water bears, are microscopic creatures, which (　　　　)[7] between 0.1 mm to 1.5 mm in length. They live almost everywhere, (　　　　)[8] 6,000-meter-high mountains to 4,600 meters below the ocean's surface. They can (　　　　)[9] be found under thick ice and in (　　　　)[10] springs. Most live in water, but (　　　　)[11] tardigrades can be found in some (　　　　)[12] the driest places on earth. One researcher reported finding tardigrades living under rocks in a desert without (　　　　)[13] recorded rainfall for 25 years. All they need (　　　　)[14] a few drops or a (　　　　)[15] layer of water to live in. (　　　　)[16] the water dries up, so do (　　　　)[17]. They lose all but three percent (　　　　)[18] their body's water and their metabolism slows down to 0.01% of (　　　　)[19] normal speed. The dried-out tardigrade is now in (　　　　)[20] state called "tun," a kind of deep sleep. (　　　　)[21] will continue in this state until it (　　　　)[22] once again soaked in water. Then, like (　　　　)[23] sponge, it absorbs the water and springs back (　　　　)[24] life again as if nothing had happened. Whether (　　　　)[25] tardigrade is in tun for 1 week (　　　　)[26] 10 years does not really matter. The moment it (　　　　)[27] surrounded by water, it comes alive again. When tardigrades are (   )²⁸ a state of tun, they are (   )²⁹ tough that they can survive in temperatures (   )³⁰ low as $-272℃$ and as (   )³¹ as $151℃$. Exactly how they achieve this (   )³² still not fully understood. Perhaps even more amazing than their ability (   )³³ survive on earth—they have been (   )³⁴ earth for some 540 million years—is their ability to survive (   )³⁵ space. In 2007, a team of European researchers (   )³⁶ a number of living tardigrades into space on (   )³⁷ outside of a rocket for 10 days. (   )³⁸ their return to earth, the researchers were surprised to (   )³⁹ that 68% were still alive.

MET 2023 本（5）日本語訳

問題英文の日本語訳を確認しよう。

世界で最もタフな動物の名前を尋ねてみれば，こう答える人がいるかもしれない。フタコブラクダ，それは，50℃もの高温でも生き残ることができる，または，北極キツネ，それは，−58℃以下の温度でも生き残ることができる。しかしながら，どちらの答えも間違っている。というのも，次のことが広く信じられているからだ。それは，クマムシが地球上で最もタフな生き物であるということだ。クマムシは，「water bear」としても知られているが，微細な生き物で，体長が0.1 mmから1.5 mmだ。クマムシは，ほぼどこにでも生息している。標高6,000メートルの山から海面下4,600メートルまで。厚い氷の下や温泉でも見つかることがある。ほとんどのクマムシは水中に生息しているが，一部のクマムシは地球上で最も乾燥した場所で見つけることができる。ある研究者は，次のような報告をした。クマムシが，25年間降水量の記録がなかった砂漠の岩の下に生息しているのを発見したと。クマムシが生きるために必要なのは，数滴の水，あるいは，水の薄い層だけだ。水が枯れると，彼らも同様に枯れる。クマムシは，体内の水分の3パーセントを除いてすべてを失い，代謝は通常の速度の0.01パーセントに低下する。干上がったクマムシは，「タン」と呼ばれる状態にある。それは，「冬眠」のような一種の深い眠りである。この状態は，ずっと続く。再度水に浸されるまで。そしてスポンジのように水を吸収し，何事もなかったかのように再び生き返る。クマムシがタンの状態にあるのが，1週間か10年かは，あまり問題ではない。水に包まれた瞬間，再び生き返るので。クマムシがタン状態にある時は，極度に丈夫で，−272℃の低温でも，151℃の高温でも生きられる。彼らがどのようにしてこれを成し遂げているのかは，まだ完全には理解されていない。おそらく，彼らの地球上での生存能力よりもさらに驚くべきことは，実際，クマムシは，約5億4千万年もの間地球上に存在してきたのだが，宇宙での生存能力だ。2007年，ヨーロッパの研究チームは，多数の生きたクマムシをロケットの外側に乗せて，宇宙に10日間送り込んだ。研究者たちは，驚いた。クマムシが，地球に戻った際に，その68％がまだ生き残っているのを見て。

MET 2023 本 (5) 解答

解答付き英文を見ながら，英語の音声をもう一度聞いてみよう。

Ask someone to name the world's toughest animal, (**and**)[1] they might say the Bactrian camel as (**it**)[2] can survive in temperatures as high (**as**)[3] 50℃, or the Arctic fox which can survive (**in**)[4] temperatures lower than −58℃. However, both answers would be wrong as (**it**)[5] is widely believed that the tardigrade is (**the**)[6] toughest creature on earth. Tardigrades, also known as water bears, are microscopic creatures, which (**are**)[7] between 0.1 mm to 1.5 mm in length. They live almost everywhere, (**from**)[8] 6,000-meter-high mountains to 4,600 meters below the ocean's surface. They can (**even**)[9] be found under thick ice and in (**hot**)[10] springs. Most live in water, but (**some**)[11] tardigrades can be found in some (**of**)[12] the driest places on earth. One researcher reported finding tardigrades living under rocks in a desert without (**any**)[13] recorded rainfall for 25 years. All they need (**are**)[14] a few drops or a (**thin**)[15] layer of water to live in. (**When**)[16] the water dries up, so do (**they**)[17]. They lose all but three percent (**of**)[18] their body's water and their metabolism slows down to 0.01% of (**its**)[19] normal speed. The dried-out tardigrade is now in (**a**)[20] state called "tun," a kind of deep sleep. (**It**)[21] will continue in this state until it (**is**)[22] once again soaked in water. Then, like (**a**)[23] sponge, it absorbs the water and springs back (**to**)[24] life again as if nothing had happened. Whether (**the**)[25] tardigrade is in tun for 1 week (**or**)[26] 10 years does not really matter. The moment it (**is**)[27] surrounded by water, it comes alive again. When tardigrades are (**in**)[28] a state of tun, they are (**so**)[29] tough that they can survive in temperatures (**as**)[30] low as −272℃ and as (**high**)[31] as 151℃. Exactly how they achieve this (**is**)[32] still not fully understood. Perhaps even more amazing than their ability (**to**)[33] survive on earth—they have been (**on**)[34] earth for some 540 million years—is their ability to survive (**in**)[35] space. In 2007, a team of European researchers (**sent**)[36] a number of living tardigrades into space on (**the**)[37] outside of a rocket for 10 days. (**On**)[38] their return to earth, the researchers were surprised to (**see**)[39] that 68% were still alive.

MET 2023 本 (6)

英語の音声を聞きながら，（　　）の中に，英単語を入れてください。

This means that for 10 days (　　　　)[1] were able to survive X-rays and ultraviolet radiation 1,000 times (　　　　)[2] intense than here on earth. Later, in 2019, (　　　　)[3] Israeli spacecraft crashed onto the moon and thousands (　　　　)[4] tardigrades in a state of tun were spilled (　　　　)[5] its surface. Whether these are still alive or not (　　　　)[6] unknown as no one has gone (　　　　)[7] collect them—which is a pity. Tardigrades are shaped (　　　　)[8] a short cucumber. They have four short legs (　　　　)[9] each side of their bodies. Some species (　　　　)[10] sticky pads at the end (　　　　)[11] each leg, while others have claws. There are 16 known (　　　　)[12] variations, which help identify those species with claws. All tardigrades have (　　　　)[13] place for eyes, but not (　　　　)[14] species have eyes. Their eyes are primitive, (　　　　)[15] having five cells in total—just one of which is light sensitive. Basically, tardigrades (　　　　)[16] be divided into those that eat plant matter, (　　　　)[17] those that eat other creatures. Those that eat vegetation (　　　　)[18] a ventral mouth—a mouth located in the lower (　　　　)[19] of the head, like (　　　　)[20] shark. The type that eats other creatures (　　　　)[21] a terminal mouth, which means the mouth is at (　　　　)[22] very front of the head, (　　　　)[23] a tuna. The mouths of tardigrades (　　　　)[24] not have teeth. They do, however, (　　　　)[25] two sharp needles, called stylets, that they use to pierce plant cells (　　　　)[26] the bodies of smaller creatures so the contents (　　　　)[27] be sucked out. Both types of tardigrades (　　　　)[28] rather simple digestive systems. The mouth leads to the pharynx (throat), where digestive juices and (   )^{29} are mixed. Located above the pharynx is a salivary gland.   (   )^{30} produces the juices that flow into (   )^{31} mouth and help with digestion. After the pharynx, there (   )^{32} a tube which transports food toward the (   )^{33}. This tube is called the esophagus. (   )^{34} middle gut, a simple stomach/ intestine type of organ, digests (   )^{35} food and absorbs the nutrients. The leftovers (   )^{36} eventually move through to the anus.

MET 2023 本（6）日本語訳

問題英文の日本語訳を確認しよう。

これは，次のことを意味する。10 日間，クマムシが，X 線や紫外線に耐えることができたということだ。X 線や紫外線は，地球上の 1,000 倍強いのにもかかわらず。その後，2019 年にイスラエルの宇宙船が月面に衝突し，数千匹のクマムシが，タンの状態で月面に放出された。そのクマムシが生きているかどうかは不明だ。といのも，誰も採集に行っていないので。これは，残念なことだ。クマムシは，短いキュウリのような形をしている。体の両側に 4 本の短い足がある。各脚の先に粘着性の肉球のようなものを持っているものや，爪を持っているものもいる。爪のバリエーションは 16 種類あることが知られており，爪がある種をそれぞれ識別するのに役立つ。すべてのクマムシには目の場所があるが，すべての種に目があるわけではない。クマムシの目は原始的で，合計 5 つの細胞しかなく，そのうちの 1 つだけが光に敏感である。基本的に，クマムシは植物を食べるものと他の生き物を食べるものに分けられる。植物を食べるものは，口が腹側にある。つまり，サメのように，頭の下部にある口を持っている。他の生き物を食べるタイプは，口が末端にある。つまり，マグロのように，頭の一番前に口がある。クマムシの口には歯がない。しかし，クマムシは，2 本の鋭い針を持っている。それは，スタイレットと呼ばれている。そして，それを使って植物の細胞や小さな生き物の体に穴を開け，内容物を吸い出している。どちらのタイプのクマムシも，かなり単純な消化器系を持っている。口は咽頭（のど）につながり，そこで消化液と食物が混ぜ合わされる。咽頭の上には唾液腺がある。これによって，液体が作られ，口の中に流れ込み，消化を助ける。咽頭の後には，管があり，食物を腸に運ぶ。この管は食道と呼ばれる。中腸は単純な胃／腸のタイプの器官で，食物を消化し，栄養素を吸収する。残りは，最終的に肛門に移動する。

MET 2023 本 (6) 解答

解答付き英文を見ながら，英語の音声をもう一度聞いてみよう。

This means that for 10 days (**most**)[1] were able to survive X-rays and ultraviolet radiation 1,000 times (**more**)[2] intense than here on earth. Later, in 2019, (**an**)[3] Israeli spacecraft crashed onto the moon and thousands (**of**)[4] tardigrades in a state of tun were spilled (**onto**)[5] its surface. Whether these are still alive or not (**is**)[6] unknown as no one has gone (**to**)[7] collect them—which is a pity. Tardigrades are shaped (**like**)[8] a short cucumber. They have four short legs (**on**)[9] each side of their bodies. Some species (**have**)[10] sticky pads at the end (**of**)[11] each leg, while others have claws. There are 16 known (**claw**)[12] variations, which help identify those species with claws. All tardigrades have (**a**)[13] place for eyes, but not (**all**)[14] species have eyes. Their eyes are primitive, (**only**)[15] having five cells in total—just one of which is light sensitive. Basically, tardigrades (**can**)[16] be divided into those that eat plant matter, (**and**)[17] those that eat other creatures. Those that eat vegetation (**have**)[18] a ventral mouth—a mouth located in the lower (**part**)[19] of the head, like (**a**)[20] shark. The type that eats other creatures (**has**)[21] a terminal mouth, which means the mouth is at (**the**)[22] very front of the head, (**like**)[23] a tuna. The mouths of tardigrades (**do**)[24] not have teeth. They do, however, (**have**)[25] two sharp needles, called stylets, that they use to pierce plant cells (**or**)[26] the bodies of smaller creatures so the contents (**can**)[27] be sucked out. Both types of tardigrades (**have**)[28] rather simple digestive systems. The mouth leads to the pharynx (throat), where digestive juices and (**food**)[29] are mixed. Located above the pharynx is a salivary gland. (**This**)[30] produces the juices that flow into (**the**)[31] mouth and help with digestion. After the pharynx, there (**is**)[32] a tube which transports food toward the (**gut**)[33]. This tube is called the esophagus. (**The**)[34] middle gut, a simple stomach/intestine type of organ, digests (**the**)[35] food and absorbs the nutrients. The leftovers (**then**)[36] eventually move through to the anus.

第2章

大学入学共通テスト追試験版 MET 問題

　この章には，問題が，18 題あります。全問題は，大学入学共通テスト英語追試験の読解テストの過去問題の英文を基に作られているので，MET 2021 追 (1) のように，名前が付けられています。各問題には，空所（　）があります。音声を聞きながら，（　）の中に，英単語を入れて下さい。18 題は，6 題ずつ 3 つのグループに分かれ，3 つのグループは，進むにつれ，難度が上がっています。

　1 題終わるごとに，答え合わせをすることができます。各問題の次のページには，その英文の日本語訳が，そして，その次のページには，解答が太字で示されています。答え合わせが終わったら，問題のページに戻り，点数を記入しておくことができます。

MET 2021 追（1）

英語の音声を聞きながら，（　　）の中に，英単語を入れてください。

This is the story of an American street photographer (　　　　　)[1] kept her passion for taking pictures secret until her death. (　　　　　)[2] lived her life as a caregiver, and (　　　　)[3] it had not been for the (　　　　)[4] of her belongings at an auction house, her incredible (　　　　)[5] might never have been discovered. It was 2007. (　　　　)[6] Chicago auction house was selling off the belongings of an (　　　　)[7] woman named Vivian Maier. She had stopped paying storage fees, and (　　　　)[8] the company decided to sell her things. Her belongings—mainly old photographs (　　　　)[9] negatives—were sold to three buyers: Maloof, Slattery, and Prow. Slattery thought Vivian's work was interesting (　　　　)[10] he published her photographs on a photo-sharing website in July 2008. The photographs received little attention. (　　　　)[11], in October, Maloof linked his blog to his selection of Vivian's photographs, (　　　　)[12] right away, thousands of people were viewing them. Maloof had (　　　　)[13] Vivian Maier's name with the prints, but he was unable (　　　　)[14] discover anything about her. Then an Internet search led him (　　　　)[15] a 2009 newspaper article about her death. Maloof used this information (　　　　)[16] discover more about Vivian's life, and it was (　　　　)[17] combination of Vivian's mysterious life story and her photographs that grabbed everyone's attention. Details (　　　　)[18] Vivian's life are limited for two reasons. First, since no one had interviewed (　　　　)[19] while she was alive, no one knew (　　　　)[20] she took so many photographs. Second, it is (　　　　)[21] from interviews with the family she worked for that Vivian (　　　　)[22] a very private person. She had few friends. Besides, she (   )^{23} kept her hobby a secret. Vivian was born (   )^{24} 1926 in the United States to an Austrian father and a French mother. (   )^{25} marriage was not a happy one, and it (   )^{26} her mother and father lived apart for several years.

MET 2021 追 (1) 日本語訳

問題英文の日本語訳を確認しよう。

これは，アメリカのストリート写真家の物語である。写真を撮ることへの情熱を死ぬまで秘密にし続けた写真家の。彼女は介護士として人生を送ったが，もしオークションハウスで彼女の持ち物が売られていなければ，彼女の信じられないような仕事は発見されなかったかもしれない。それは2007年のことだった。シカゴのオークションハウスは，ヴィヴィアン・マイヤーという名前の老婦人の持ち物を売りに出していた。彼女は倉庫代の支払いをやめていたため，会社は彼女の物を売却することに決めた。彼女の所有物（主に古い写真とネガ）は，3人に売却された。マルーフ，スラッテリー，そして，プラウ。スラッテリーは，ビビアンの作品はおもしろいと思い，彼女の写真を写真共有ウェブサイトに公開した。それは，2008年7月のことだった。しかし，その写真はほとんど注目されなかった。そして，その10月，マルーフは，自分のブログを，自分が作ったヴィヴィアンの写真集にリンクさせた。すると，すぐに何千人もの人がその写真を閲覧するようになった。マルーフは，紙の写真からヴィヴィアン・マイヤーの名前を見つけていたが，彼女自身については何も発見できなかった。その後，インターネット検索で2009年の新聞記事にたどり着いた。それは，ヴィヴィアンの死に関するものだった。マルーフはこの情報を利用して，ヴィヴィアンの人生についてさらに詳しく調べた。そして，ヴィヴィアンの神秘的な人生の物語と彼女の写真との組み合わせが，人の注目を集めた。ビビアンの生涯の詳細は，極めて限定されている。2つの理由で。第一に，生きている間に，ビビアンにインタビューした者は誰もいなかったので，なぜビビアンがこれほど多くの写真を撮ったのか誰もわからなかった。第二に，ビビアンが働いていた家族へのインタビューから，ヴィヴィアンが極度に人と距離をおく人間だったことがわかる。彼女には友達がほとんどいなかった。しかも，彼女は自分の趣味を秘密にしていた。ヴィヴィアンは，1926年にアメリカで生まれた。オーストリア人の父親とフランス人の母親の間に。結婚生活は決して幸せなものではなく，父親と母親は数年間別居していたようだ。

MET 2021 追（1）解答

解答付き英文を見ながら，英語の音声をもう一度聞いてみよう。

This is the story of an American street photographer (**who**)[1] kept her passion for taking pictures secret until her death. (**She**)[2] lived her life as a caregiver, and (**if**)[3] it had not been for the (**sale**)[4] of her belongings at an auction house, her incredible (**work**)[5] might never have been discovered. It was 2007. (**A**)[6] Chicago auction house was selling off the belongings of an (**old**)[7] woman named Vivian Maier. She had stopped paying storage fees, and (**so**)[8] the company decided to sell her things. Her belongings—mainly old photographs (**and**)[9] negatives—were sold to three buyers: Maloof, Slattery, and Prow. Slattery thought Vivian's work was interesting (**so**)[10] he published her photographs on a photo-sharing website in July 2008. The photographs received little attention. (**Then**)[11], in October, Maloof linked his blog to his selection of Vivian's photographs, (**and**)[12] right away, thousands of people were viewing them. Maloof had (**found**)[13] Vivian Maier's name with the prints, but he was unable (**to**)[14] discover anything about her. Then an Internet search led him (**to**)[15] a 2009 newspaper article about her death. Maloof used this information (**to**)[16] discover more about Vivian's life, and it was (**the**)[17] combination of Vivian's mysterious life story and her photographs that grabbed everyone's attention. Details (**of**)[18] Vivian's life are limited for two reasons. First, since no one had interviewed (**her**)[19] while she was alive, no one knew (**why**)[20] she took so many photographs. Second, it is (**clear**)[21] from interviews with the family she worked for that Vivian (**was**)[22] a very private person. She had few friends. Besides, she (**had**)[23] kept her hobby a secret. Vivian was born (**in**)[24] 1926 in the United States to an Austrian father and a French mother. (**The**)[25] marriage was not a happy one, and it (**seems**)[26] her mother and father lived apart for several years.

MET 2021 追 (2)

英語の音声を聞きながら，（　）の中に，英単語を入れてください。

During her childhood Vivian frequently moved between the US and France, sometimes living in France, and sometimes (　　　)[1] the US. For a while, Vivian and her mother (　　　)[2] in New York with Jeanne Bertrand, a successful photographer. It is believed that Vivian became interested (　　　)[3] photography as a young adult, as her first photos (　　　)[4] taken in France in the late 1940s using (　　　)[5] very simple camera. She returned to New York in 1951, and in 1956 (　　　)[6] moved to Chicago to work as a caregiver (　　　)[7] the Gensburg family. This job gave her more (　　　)[8] time for taking photographs. In 1952, at the age (　　　)[9] 26, she purchased her first 6 x 6 camera, and it was with (　　　)[10] that most of her photographs of life (　　　)[11] the streets of Chicago were taken. For over 30 (　　　)[12] she took photos of children, the elderly, the rich, (　　　)[13] the poor. Some people were not even (　　　)[14] that their picture was being taken. She (　　　)[15] took a number of self-portraits. Some were reflections of herself (　　　)[16] a shop window. Others were of her own shadow. Vivian continued (　　　)[17] document Chicago life until the early 1970s, when she changed (　　　)[18] a new style of photography. An international award-winning documentary film called *Finding Vivian Maier* brought interest (　　　)[19] her work to a wider audience. The (　　　)[20] led to exhibitions in Europe and the US. To choose (　　　)[21] photographs that best represent her style, those in charge (　　　)[22] the exhibitions have tried to answer the question, "What (　　　)[23] Vivian Maier have printed?" In order to answer this question, they (   )[24] her notes, the photos she actually did print, (   )[25] information about her preferences as reported by the Gensburgs. Vivian was (   )[26] more interested in capturing moments rather than the outcome. So, one could (   )[27] the mystery behind Vivian's work remains largely "undeveloped."

MET 2021 追 (2) 日本語訳

問題英文の日本語訳を確認しよう。

ヴィヴィアンは，幼少期に，米国とフランスを頻繁に行き来し，時にはフランスに，時には米国に住んでいた。しばらくの間，ヴィヴィアンと母親は，ニューヨークに住んでいた。ジャンヌ・ベルトランという成功した写真家と一緒に。ヴィヴィアンは，若い頃に写真に興味を持ったと考えられている。というのも，彼女の最初の写真が 1940 年代後半にフランスで撮影されていたからである。その写真は，非常に単純なカメラで撮影された。彼女は，1951 年にニューヨークに戻り，1956 年にシカゴに移った。ゲンスバーグ家で介護士として働くために。この仕事のおかげで，彼女は，写真を撮るための自由時間が増えた。1952 年，26 歳の時，彼女は最初の 6 x 6 カメラを購入した。シカゴの路上での生活の写真のほとんどは，これで撮影された。30 年以上にわたり，彼女は，子供，高齢者，富裕層，貧困層の写真を撮り続けた。自分の写真が撮られていることに気づいていない人もいた。彼女はまた，何枚もの自画像を撮った。ショーウィンドウに映った自分自身の姿もあった。自分自身の影の写真もあった。ヴィヴィアンは，1970 年代初頭までシカゴの生活を記録し続け，その後，新しいスタイルの写真に切り替えた。国際的な賞を受賞したドキュメンタリー映画『Finding Vivian Maier』によって，より幅広い視聴者が，彼女の作品に関心を持つようになった。この映画のおかげで，ヨーロッパとアメリカで展覧会が開かれることになった。彼女のスタイルを最もよく表す写真を選ぼうと，展覧会の担当者は，次のような疑問に答えようとした。「ヴィヴィアン・マイヤーだったらどの写真を印刷しただろうか？」この疑問に答えるために，彼らは，彼女のメモ，彼女が実際に印刷した写真，ゲンスブルク家が報告してくれた彼女の好みに関する情報を利用した。ヴィヴィアンは，瞬間を捉えることにずっと興味を持っていた。結果よりも。したがって，こういう結論になるであろう。ヴィヴィアンの作品の背後にある謎は，ほとんど「未解明」のままであるという。

MET 2021 追 (2) 解答

解答付き英文を見ながら，英語の音声をもう一度聞いてみよう。

During her childhood Vivian frequently moved between the US and France, sometimes living in France, and sometimes (**in**)^1 the US. For a while, Vivian and her mother (**lived**)^2 in New York with Jeanne Bertrand, a successful photographer. It is believed that Vivian became interested (**in**)^3 photography as a young adult, as her first photos (**were**)^4 taken in France in the late 1940s using (**a**)^5 very simple camera. She returned to New York in 1951, and in 1956 (**she**)^6 moved to Chicago to work as a caregiver (**for**)^7 the Gensburg family. This job gave her more (**free**)^8 time for taking photographs. In 1952, at the age (**of**)^9 26, she purchased her first 6 x 6 camera, and it was with (**this**)^{10} that most of her photographs of life (**on**)^{11} the streets of Chicago were taken. For over 30 (**years**)^{12} she took photos of children, the elderly, the rich, (**and**)^{13} the poor. Some people were not even (**aware**)^{14} that their picture was being taken. She (**also**)^{15} took a number of self-portraits. Some were reflections of herself (**in**)^{16} a shop window. Others were of her own shadow. Vivian continued (**to**)^{17} document Chicago life until the early 1970s, when she changed (**to**)^{18} a new style of photography. An international award-winning documentary film called *Finding Vivian Maier* brought interest (**in**)^{19} her work to a wider audience. The (**film**)^{20} led to exhibitions in Europe and the US. To choose (**the**)^{21} photographs that best represent her style, those in charge (**of**)^{22} the exhibitions have tried to answer the question, "What (**would**)^{23} Vivian Maier have printed?" In order to answer this question, they (**used**)^{24} her notes, the photos she actually did print, (**and**)^{25} information about her preferences as reported by the Gensburgs. Vivian was (**much**)^{26} more interested in capturing moments rather than the outcome. So, one could (**say**)^{27} the mystery behind Vivian's work remains largely "undeveloped."

MET 2021 追 (3)

英語の音声を聞きながら，（　　　）の中に，英単語を入れてください。

We are all different. While most people recognize that (　　　　)[1] world is made up of a (　　　　)[2] variety of people, diversity—showing and accepting our differences—is often not reflected (　　　　)[3] performing arts organizations. For this reason, there is an increasing demand (　　　　)[4] movies and plays to better represent people from various backgrounds as well (　　　　)[5] those with disabilities. Arts Council England, in response to this demand, is encouraging (　　　　)[6] publicly funded arts organizations to make improvements in this area. One theater company responding positively (　　　　)[7] the Royal Shakespeare Company (RSC), which is one of the most influential theater companies (　　　　)[8] the world. Based in Stratford-upon-Avon in the UK, (　　　　)[9] RSC produces plays by William Shakespeare and a number of other famous authors. (　　　　)[10] days, the RSC is focused on diversity in an attempt (　　　　)[11] represent all of UK society accurately. It works hard to balance (　　　　)[12] ethnic and social backgrounds, the genders, and the physical abilities of both performers (　　　　)[13] staff when hiring. During the summer 2019 season, the RSC put on three (　　　　)[14] Shakespeare's comedies: *As You Like It*, *The Taming of the Shrew*, and *Measure for Measure*. Actors from all over the country were employed, forming (　　　　)[15] 27-member cast, reflecting the diverse ethnic, geographical, and cultural population of the UK today. (　　　　)[16] achieve gender balance for the entire season, half of all roles (　　　　)[17] given to male actors and half to female actors.

MET 2021 追 (3) 日本語訳

問題英文の日本語訳を確認しよう。

私たちは，それぞれ，皆違う。世界は多種多様な人々で構成されていることをほとんどの人が認識しているが，多様性，つまり違いを示し，受け入れることは，反映されていないことがよくある。舞台芸術団体においては。このため，映画や演劇に対するこんな需要が高まっている。障害がある人だけでなく，さまざまな背景を持つ人をよりよく表現する，そんな映画や演劇だ。イングランド芸術評議会は，この要求に応えて，すべての公的資金による芸術団体に，この分野の改善を奨励している。劇団の一つが，肯定的な反応を示している。それは，ロイヤルシェイクスピアカンパニー(RSC) だ。RSC は，世界で最も影響力のある劇団の1つである。RSC は，英国のストラトフォード - アポン - エイボンに拠点を置き，演劇を制作している。ウィリアム・シェイクスピアやその他の多くの有名な作家による演劇だ。最近，RSC は，多様性に焦点を当てている。英国社会全体を正確に表現するために。採用にあたっては，出演者とスタッフ双方の民族的・社会的背景，性別，身体能力などのバランスを考慮している。2019 年の夏のシーズン中，RSC はシェイクスピアのコメディを3本上演した。それは，『お気に召すまま』，『じゃじゃ馬ならし』，『メジャー・フォー・メジャー』である。全国から俳優が起用され，27 人のキャストが形成された。キャストは，今日の英国の多様な民族，地理，文化を反映したものだ。シーズン全体で男女のバランスを保つため，全役柄の半分は男性俳優に，半分は女性俳優に割り当てられた。

MET 2021 追 (3) 解答

解答付き英文を見ながら，英語の音声をもう一度聞いてみよう。

We are all different. While most people recognize that (**the**)[1] world is made up of a (**wide**)[2] variety of people, diversity—showing and accepting our differences—is often not reflected (**in**)[3] performing arts organizations. For this reason, there is an increasing demand (**for**)[4] movies and plays to better represent people from various backgrounds as well (**as**)[5] those with disabilities. Arts Council England, in response to this demand, is encouraging (**all**)[6] publicly funded arts organizations to make improvements in this area. One theater company responding positively (**is**)[7] the Royal Shakespeare Company (RSC), which is one of the most influential theater companies (**in**)[8] the world. Based in Stratford-upon-Avon in the UK, (**the**)[9] RSC produces plays by William Shakespeare and a number of other famous authors. (**These**)[10] days, the RSC is focused on diversity in an attempt (**to**)[11] represent all of UK society accurately. It works hard to balance (**the**)[12] ethnic and social backgrounds, the genders, and the physical abilities of both performers (**and**)[13] staff when hiring. During the summer 2019 season, the RSC put on three (**of**)[14] Shakespeare's comedies: *As You Like It*, *The Taming of the Shrew*, and *Measure for Measure*. Actors from all over the country were employed, forming (**a**)[15] 27-member cast, reflecting the diverse ethnic, geographical, and cultural population of the UK today. (**To**)[16] achieve gender balance for the entire season, half of all roles (**were**)[17] given to male actors and half to female actors.

音声 Track **22**

MET 2021 追 (4)

／ 18 点

英語の音声を聞きながら，（　　）の中に，英単語を入れてください。

The cast included three actors with disabilities (currently referred to as "differently-abled" actors)—one visually-impaired, one hearing-impaired, and one (　　　　)[1] a wheelchair. Changes went beyond the hiring policy. The RSC actually rewrote parts of (　　　　)[2] plays to encourage the audience to reflect on male/female power relationships. (　　　　)[3] example, female and male roles were reversed. In *The Taming of the Shrew*, the (　　　　)[4] of "the daughter" in the original was transformed into "the son" and played (　　　　)[5] a male actor. In the same (　　　　)[6], a male servant character was rewritten as a female servant. That (　　　　)[7] was played by Amy Trigg, a female actor who uses (　　　　)[8] wheelchair. Trigg said that she was excited to play (　　　　)[9] role and believed that the RSC's changes would have (　　　　)[10] large impact on other performing arts organizations. Excited by all (　　　　)[11] diversity, other members of the RSC expressed the same hope—(　　　　)[12] more arts organizations would be encouraged to follow in (　　　　)[13] RSC's footsteps. The RSC's decision to reflect diversity in the summer 2019 season can be (　　　　)[14] as a new mode for arts organizations hoping (　　　　)[15] make their organizations inclusive. While there are some (　　　　)[16] are reluctant to accept diversity in classic plays, others welcome it with (　　　　)[17] arms. Although certain challenges remain, the RSC has earned its reputation as the (　　　　)[18] of progress.

91

MET 2021 追（4）日本語訳

問題英文の日本語訳を確認しよう。

キャストには，障害がある俳優（現在は「異なる能力を持つ」俳優と呼ばれている）が 3 人含まれていた。そのうち 1 人は視覚障害者，1 人は聴覚障害者，1 人は車椅子に乗っていた。こういった雇用政策を超える変化もあった。RSC は，実際，劇の一部を書き直しさえし，観客が，男性と女性の力関係について熟考するよう促した。例えば，女性と男性の役割を逆転させたりした。『じゃじゃ馬ならし』では，原作の「娘」の役が「息子」に変えられ，男性俳優が演じた。同劇では，男性の使用人役が女性の使用人として書き直された。その役を演じたのはエイミー・トリッグだった。車椅子を使用する女性俳優だ。トリッグは，語った。この役を演じることに興奮しており，RSC の変更は他の舞台芸術団体に大きな影響を与えると信じていると。RSC の他のメンバーも，その多様性に興奮し，同様の希望を表明した。より多くの芸術団体が，奨励され，RSC の足跡をたどるようにという希望だ。RSC の決定，それは，2019 年夏のシーズンに多様性を反映させるという決定であるが，芸術団体にとっての新しいモデルと見なすことができる。組織を包括的なものにしたいと考えている芸術団体にとってのモデルだ。古典劇に多様性を受け入れることに消極的な人もいるが，両手を広げて歓迎する人もいる。いくつかの課題は残っているが，RSC は進歩の顔としての評判を獲得している。

MET 2021 追 (4) 解答

解答付き英文を見ながら，英語の音声をもう一度聞いてみよう。

The cast included three actors with disabilities (currently referred to as "differently-abled" actors) —one visually-impaired, one hearing-impaired, and one (**in**)[1] a wheelchair. Changes went beyond the hiring policy. The RSC actually rewrote parts of (**the**)[2] plays to encourage the audience to reflect on male/female power relationships. (**For**)[3] example, female and male roles were reversed. In *The Taming of the Shrew*, the (**role**)[4] of "the daughter" in the original was transformed into "the son" and played (**by**)[5] a male actor. In the same (**play**)[6], a male servant character was rewritten as a female servant. That (**role**)[7] was played by Amy Trigg, a female actor who uses (**a**)[8] wheelchair. Trigg said that she was excited to play (**the**)[9] role and believed that the RSC's changes would have (**a**)[10] large impact on other performing arts organizations. Excited by all (**the**)[11] diversity, other members of the RSC expressed the same hope—(**that**)[12] more arts organizations would be encouraged to follow in (**the**)[13] RSC's footsteps. The RSC's decision to reflect diversity in the summer 2019 season can be (**seen**)[14] as a new mode for arts organizations hoping (**to**)[15] make their organizations inclusive. While there are some (**who**)[16] are reluctant to accept diversity in classic plays, others welcome it with (**open**)[17] arms. Although certain challenges remain, the RSC has earned its reputation as the (**face**)[18] of progress.

英語の音声を聞きながら，（　）の中に，英単語を入れてください。

In recent years, governments around the world have been working (   )[1] raise awareness about oral health. While many people have (   )[2] that brushing their teeth multiple times per day (   )[3] a good habit, they most likely have (   )[4] considered all the reasons why this is crucial. Simply stated, teeth (   )[5] important. Teeth are required to pronounce words accurately. In fact, (   )[6] oral health can actually make it difficult to speak. (   )[7] even more basic necessity is being able (   )[8] chew well. Chewing breaks food down and makes (   )[9] easier for the body to digest it. Proper chewing is (   )[10] linked to the enjoyment of food. The average person has experienced (   )[11] frustration of not being able to chew (   )[12] one side after a dental procedure. A person with weak (   )[13] may experience this disappointment all the time. In (   )[14] words, oral health impacts people's quality of life. While the (   )[15] functions of teeth are clear, many people do (   )[16] realize that the mouth provides a mirror for the (   )[17]. Research shows that good oral health is a (   )[18] sign of good general health. People with poor oral health (   )[19] more likely to develop serious physical diseases. Ignoring recommended daily oral health routines can have negative effects (   )[20] those already suffering from diseases. Conversely, practicing good oral health may even prevent disease. (   )[21] strong, healthy body is often a reflection of a (   )[22], well-maintained mouth. Maintaining good oral health is a lifelong mission. The Finnish (   )[23] US governments recommend that parents take their infants to the dentist before the (   )^{24} turns one year old. Finland actually sends parents notices. New Zealand offers free dental treatment to everyone (   )^{25} to age 18. The Japanese government promotes an 8020 (Eighty-Twenty) Campaign. As people age, (   )^{26} can lose teeth for various reasons. The goal (   )^{27} the campaign is still to have at (   )^{28} 20 teeth in the mouth on one's 80th birthday.

MET 2021 追（5）日本語訳

問題英文の日本語訳を確認しよう。

近年，世界中の政府が，意識を高めることに取り組んでいる。口腔の健康に対する意識だ。多くの人は，一日に複数回歯を磨くのは，いい習慣だと聞いたことはあるが，なぜこれが重要なのか考えたことはないだろう。一言で言えば，歯は大切だ。歯は，言葉を正確に発音するために必要だ。もっと言うと，口腔の健康状態が悪いと，実際に話すことが困難になる。さらに基本的に必要なことは，よく噛むことだ。噛むことで食べ物が分解され，体が消化しやすくなる。正しく噛むことは，食事を楽しむことにもつながる。普通に暮らしている人なら，歯の治療後に，片側で噛めなくなるといういらいら感を経験したことがあるだろう。歯が弱い人は，このようながっかり感を常に経験するかもしれない。言い換えれば，口腔の健康は人々の生活の質に影響を与える。歯の基本的な機能は明らかであるが，口が体の鏡となっていることに多くの人は気付いていない。研究によると，口腔の健康状態が良好であることは，全身の健康状態が良好であることを明確に示している。口腔の健康状態が悪い人は，重篤な身体疾患を発症する可能性が高くなる。推奨されている毎日の口腔衛生習慣を無視すると，すでに病気に苦しんでいる人に悪影響を与える可能性がある。逆に，口腔の健康を維持することで病気を予防できる可能性もある。強くて健康な体は，多くの場合，清潔で手入れの行き届いた口の状態を反映している。口腔の健康を維持することは，生涯にわたる使命だ。フィンランドと米国の政府は，次のことを推奨している。親が乳児を歯医者に連れて行くことだ。乳児が1歳になる前に。フィンランドでは，実際に保護者に通知を送っている。ニュージーランドでは，18歳までの歯科治療が無料となっている。日本政府は8020（エイティ・トゥエンティ）キャンペーンを推進している。人は年齢を重ねると，さまざまな理由で歯を失うことがある。このキャンペーンの目標は，口の中に少なくとも20本の歯が残っているようにすることだ。80歳の誕生日に。

MET 2021 追（5）解答

解答付き英文を見ながら，英語の音声をもう一度聞いてみよう。

In recent years, governments around the world have been working (**to**)¹ raise awareness about oral health. While many people have (**heard**)² that brushing their teeth multiple times per day (**is**)³ a good habit, they most likely have (**not**)⁴ considered all the reasons why this is crucial. Simply stated, teeth (**are**)⁵ important. Teeth are required to pronounce words accurately. In fact, (**poor**)⁶ oral health can actually make it difficult to speak. (**An**)⁷ even more basic necessity is being able (**to**)⁸ chew well. Chewing breaks food down and makes (**it**)⁹ easier for the body to digest it. Proper chewing is (**also**)¹⁰ linked to the enjoyment of food. The average person has experienced (**the**)¹¹ frustration of not being able to chew (**on**)¹² one side after a dental procedure. A person with weak (**teeth**)¹³ may experience this disappointment all the time. In (**other**)¹⁴ words, oral health impacts people's quality of life. While the (**basic**)¹⁵ functions of teeth are clear, many people do (**not**)¹⁶ realize that the mouth provides a mirror for the (**body**)¹⁷. Research shows that good oral health is a (**clear**)¹⁸ sign of good general health. People with poor oral health (**are**)¹⁹ more likely to develop serious physical diseases. Ignoring recommended daily oral health routines can have negative effects (**on**)²⁰ those already suffering from diseases. Conversely, practicing good oral health may even prevent disease. (**A**)²¹ strong, healthy body is often a reflection of a (**clean**)²², well-maintained mouth. Maintaining good oral health is a lifelong mission. The Finnish (**and**)²³ US governments recommend that parents take their infants to the dentist before the (**baby**)²⁴ turns one year old. Finland actually sends parents notices. New Zealand offers free dental treatment to everyone (**up**)²⁵ to age 18. The Japanese government promotes an 8020 (Eighty-Twenty) Campaign. As people age, (**they**)²⁶ can lose teeth for various reasons. The goal (**of**)²⁷ the campaign is still to have at (**least**)²⁸ 20 teeth in the mouth on one's 80th birthday.

MET 2021 追（6）

英語の音声を聞きながら，（　　）の中に，英単語を入れてください。

Taking a closer look at Japan, the Ministry of Health, Labour and Welfare has been analyzing survey (　　　　)¹ on the number of remaining teeth in seniors for (　　　　)² years. One researcher divided the oldest participants into four age groups: A (70–74), B (75–79), C (80–84), and D (85+). In (　　　　)³ survey, with the exception of 1993, the percentages of people with (　　　　)⁴ least 20 teeth were in A-B-C-D order from (　　　　)⁵ to low. Between 1993 and 1999, however, Group A improved only about six percentage points, while (　　　　)⁶ increase for B was slightly higher. In 1993, 25.5% in Group A had at (　　　　)⁷ 20 teeth, but by 2016 the Group D percentage was actually 0.2 percentage points higher than Group A's initial figure. Group B increased steadily (　　　　)⁸ first, but went up dramatically between 2005 and 2011. Thanks to better awareness, every (　　　　)⁹ has improved significantly over the years. Dentists have long recommended brushing (　　　　)¹⁰ meals. People actively seeking excellent oral health may brush several times per (　　　　)¹¹. Most brush their teeth before they go (　　　　)¹² sleep and then again at some (　　　　)¹³ the following morning. Dentists also believe it is important to floss (　　　　)¹⁴, using a special type of string to remove substances from between (　　　　)¹⁵. Another prevention method is for a dentist to seal the (　　　　)¹⁶ using a plastic gel (sealant) that hardens around the (　　　　)¹⁷ surface and prevents damage. Sealant is gaining popularity especially for use with children. This (　　　　)¹⁸ takes one coating and prevents an amazing 80% of common dental problems. Visiting the dentist annually or (   )[19] frequently is key. As dental treatment sometimes causes pain, there are (   )[20] who actively avoid seeing a dentist. However, it is important that people (   )[21] viewing their dentist as an important ally who can, literally, (   )[22] them smile throughout their lives.

MET 2021 追 (6) 日本語訳

問題英文の日本語訳を確認しよう。

日本に目を向けると，厚生労働省は長年，調査データを分析してきた。高齢者の残存歯数に関する調査データだ。ある研究者は，最高齢の参加者を 4 つの年齢グループに分けた。A（70 ～ 74 歳），B（75 ～ 79 歳），C（80 ～ 84 歳），D（85 歳以上）だ。1993 年を除く各調査では，少なくとも 20 本の歯を持つ人の割合は，高い方から低い方へ，A–B–C–D の順だった。しかし，1993 年から 1999 年の間に，グループ A は約 6 パーセントしか改善しなかったのに対し，グループ B の増加はわずかに大きかった。1993 年には，グループ A の 25.5% は，少なくとも 20 本の歯を持っていたが，2016 年までに，グループ D の割合は，実際には，0.2 パーセント高かった。グループ A の当初の数字よりも。グループ B は，初めは着実に増加していたが，2005 年から 2011 年にかけて劇的に増加した。認識の向上のおかげで，どのグループも長年にわたって大幅に改善した。歯科医は長い間，食後の歯磨きを推奨してきた。優れた口腔の健康を積極的に求めるなら，1 日に数回歯を磨く人もいる。ほとんどの人は，寝る前に歯を磨き，翌朝のある時点でもう一度歯を磨く。歯科医はまた，フロスを毎日行うことが重要であると考えている。フロスとは，特殊な種類の紐を使用して，歯の間の物質を取り除くことだ。もう一つの予防方法は，歯科医が歯を密閉することだ。プラスチックゲル（シーラント）を使用ながら，歯の表面を硬化させて損傷を防ぐという方法だ。シーラントは，人気が高まっている。特に子供向けに。たった 1 回のコーティングで，一般的な歯の問題の 80% を防ぐ。驚くべき数字だ。毎年，またはそれ以上の頻度で歯科医を訪問することがカギとなる。歯科治療には痛みを伴うことがあるため，歯医者に受診するのをわざわざ避ける人もいる。しかしながら，人々が，こう考えるようになることが重要だ。歯科医は，重要な味方で，文字通り，生涯を通じて笑顔でいさせてくれるということだ。

MET 2021 追（6）解答

解答付き英文を見ながら，英語の音声をもう一度聞いてみよう。

Taking a closer look at Japan, the Ministry of Health, Labour and Welfare has been analyzing survey（ **data** ）[1] on the number of remaining teeth in seniors for（ **many** ）[2] years. One researcher divided the oldest participants into four age groups: A（70-74）, B（75-79）, C（80-84）, and D（85+）. In（ **each** ）[3] survey, with the exception of 1993, the percentages of people with（ **at** ）[4] least 20 teeth were in A-B-C-D order from（ **high** ）[5] to low. Between 1993 and 1999, however, Group A improved only about six percentage points, while（ **the** ）[6] increase for B was slightly higher. In 1993, 25.5% in Group A had at（ **least** ）[7] 20 teeth, but by 2016 the Group D percentage was actually 0.2 percentage points higher than Group A's initial figure. Group B increased steadily（ **at** ）[8] first, but went up dramatically between 2005 and 2011. Thanks to better awareness, every（ **group** ）[9] has improved significantly over the years. Dentists have long recommended brushing（ **after** ）[10] meals. People actively seeking excellent oral health may brush several times per（ **day** ）[11]. Most brush their teeth before they go（ **to** ）[12] sleep and then again at some（ **time** ）[13] the following morning. Dentists also believe it is important to floss（ **daily** ）[14], using a special type of string to remove substances from between（ **teeth** ）[15]. Another prevention method is for a dentist to seal the（ **teeth** ）[16] using a plastic gel（sealant）that hardens around the（ **tooth** ）[17] surface and prevents damage. Sealant is gaining popularity especially for use with children. This（ **only** ）[18] takes one coating and prevents an amazing 80% of common dental problems. Visiting the dentist annually or（ **more** ）[19] frequently is key. As dental treatment sometimes causes pain, there are（ **those** ）[20] who actively avoid seeing a dentist. However, it is important that people（ **start** ）[21] viewing their dentist as an important ally who can, literally,（ **make** ）[22] them smile throughout their lives.

MET 2022 追 (1)

英語の音声を聞きながら，（　）の中に，英単語を入れてください。

During his 87 years of life, both (　　　　　)[1] and below the waves, Jacques Cousteau did (　　　　)[2] great things.　He was an officer in (　　　　)[3] French navy, an explorer, an environmentalist, a filmmaker, a scientist, (　　　　)[4] author, and a researcher who studied all forms (　　　　)[5] underwater life.　Born in France in 1910, he (　　　　)[6] to school in Paris and then entered the French (　　　　)[7] academy in 1930.　After graduating in 1933, he was training (　　　　)[8] become a pilot, when he was involved (　　　　)[9] a car accident and was badly injured.　(　　　　)[10] put an end to his flying career.　(　　　　)[11] help recover from his injuries, Cousteau began swimming in (　　　　)[12] Mediterranean, which increased his interest in life underwater.　Around this (　　　　)[13], he carried out his first underwater research.　Cousteau remained in the (　　　　)[14] until 1949, even though he could no longer follow (　　　　)[15] dream of becoming a pilot. In (　　　　)[16] 1940s, Cousteau became friends with Marcel Ichac, who lived in the (　　　　)[17] village.　Both men shared a desire to explore unknown and difficult-to-reach places.　(　　　　)[18] Ichac this was mountain peaks, and for Cousteau (　　　　)[19] was the mysterious world under the (　　　　)[20].　In 1943, these two neighbors became widely recognized when they won (　　　　)[21] prize for the first French underwater documentary.　Their documentary, *18 Meters Deep*, had (　　　　)[22] filmed the previous year without breathing equipment.　After their success they (　　　　)[23] on to make another film, *Shipwrecks*, using one (　　　　)[24] the very first underwater breathing devices, known as the Aqua-Lung.

(　　　　)²⁵ filming *Shipwrecks*, Cousteau was not satisfied with how long

(　　　　)²⁶ could breathe underwater, and made improvements to its design. (　　　　)²⁷ improved equipment enabled him to explore the wreck

of (　　　　)²⁸ Roman ship, the *Mahdia*, in 1948. Cousteau was always

watching the (　　　　)²⁹, even from age four when he first learned

(　　　　)³⁰ to swim. In his book, *The Silent World*, published

(　　　　)³¹ 1953, he describes a group of dolphins following his

(　　　　)³².

MET 2022 追（1）日本語訳

問題英文の日本語訳を確認しよう。

87 年間の生涯で，波の上でも下でも，ジャック・クストーは，多くの偉大な功績を残した。彼は，フランス海軍の士官であり，探検家，環境活動家，映画製作者，科学者，作家であり，あらゆる形態の水中生物を研究する研究者でもあった。1910 年にフランスで生まれ，彼は，パリの学校に通い，1930 年にフランス海軍兵学校に入学した。1933 年に卒業後，パイロットになる訓練を受けていたところ，交通事故に遭い，重傷を負った。これによって，パイロットになるというキャリアに終止符が打たれた。怪我から回復するために，クストーは地中海で泳ぎ始め，それにより水中生活への関心が高まった。この頃，彼は，初めて水中での研究を行った。クストーは，1949 年まで海軍に残った。パイロットになるという夢を追うことができなくなったにもかかわらず。1940 年代に，クストーは，マルセル・イシャックと友人になった。マルセルは，同じ村に住んでいた。二人とも，こんな願望を共有していた。未知の場所や到達困難な場所を探検したいという願望だ。イシャックにとって，それは山の頂上であり，クストーにとって，それは海の下の神秘的な世界であった。1943 年，この 2 人の隣人は，広く知られるようになった。フランス初の水中ドキュメンタリーで賞を受賞したのだ。彼らのドキュメンタリー『水深 18 メートル』は，前年に撮影されていた。呼吸器を使わずに。彼らの成功の後，彼らは続けて別の映画を製作した。『難破船』だ。最初の水中呼吸装置の 1 つを使用して。それは，アクアラングとして知られている。クストーは，『難破船』の撮影中，水中でどれだけ長く呼吸できるかに満足できず，その設計に改良を加えた。改良された装置のおかげで，1948 年に，ローマの難破船マハディア号を探検することができた。クストーは，常に海を眺めていた。4 歳の時から。それは，初めて泳ぎ方を習った時だ。著書『沈黙の世界』の中で，それは，1953 年に出版されたものだが，彼は，イルカの群れについて記述している。自分のボートを追いかけるイルカの群れだ。

MET 2022 追 (1) 解答

解答付き英文を見ながら，英語の音声をもう一度聞いてみよう。

During his 87 years of life, both (**above**)[1] and below the waves, Jacques Cousteau did (**many**)[2] great things. He was an officer in (**the**)[3] French navy, an explorer, an environmentalist, a film-maker, a scientist, (**an**)[4] author, and a researcher who studied all forms (**of**)[5] underwater life. Born in France in 1910, he (**went**)[6] to school in Paris and then entered the French (**naval**)[7] academy in 1930. After graduating in 1933, he was training (**to**)[8] become a pilot, when he was involved (**in**)[9] a car accident and was badly injured. (**This**)[10] put an end to his flying career. (**To**)[11] help recover from his injuries, Cousteau began swimming in (**the**)[12] Mediterranean, which increased his interest in life underwater. Around this (**time**)[13], he carried out his first underwater research. Cousteau remained in the (**navy**)[14] until 1949, even though he could no longer follow (**his**)[15] dream of becoming a pilot. In (**the**)[16] 1940s, Cousteau became friends with Marcel Ichac, who lived in the (**same**)[17] village. Both men shared a desire to explore unknown and difficult-to-reach places. (**For**)[18] Ichac this was mountain peaks, and for Cousteau (**it**)[19] was the mysterious world under the (**sea**)[20]. In 1943, these two neighbors became widely recognized when they won (**a**)[21] prize for the first French underwater documentary. Their documentary, *18 Meters Deep*, had (**been**)[22] filmed the previous year without breathing equipment. After their success they (**went**)[23] on to make another film, *Shipwrecks*, using one (**of**)[24] the very first underwater breathing devices, known as the Aqua-Lung. (**While**)[25] filming *Shipwrecks*, Cousteau was not satisfied with how long (**he**)[26] could breathe underwater, and made improvements to its design. (**His**)[27] improved equipment enabled him to explore the wreck of (**the**)[28] Roman ship, the *Mahdia*, in 1948. Cousteau was always watching the (**ocean**)[29], even from age four when he first learned (**how**)[30] to swim. In his book, *The Silent World*, published (**in**)[31] 1953, he describes a group of dolphins following his (**boat**)[32].

MET 2022 追 (2)

英語の音声を聞きながら，（　　）の中に，英単語を入れてください。

He had long suspected that dolphins used echolocation (navigating
(　　　　)¹ sound waves), so he decided to (　　　　)² an experiment.
Cousteau changed direction by a few degrees so (　　　　)³ the boat wasn't
following the best course, according to (　　　　)⁴ underwater maps. The
dolphins followed for a few minutes, (　　　　)⁵ then changed back to their
original course. Seeing this, Cousteau confirmed (　　　　)⁶ prediction
about their ability, even though human use (　　　　)⁷ echolocation was
still relatively new. Throughout his life, Cousteau's (　　　　)⁸ would continue to be recognized internationally. He had (　　　　)⁹ ability to capture
the beauty of the world (　　　　)¹⁰ the surface of the ocean with cameras,
(　　　　)¹¹ he shared the images with ordinary people through his many
publications. (　　　　)¹² this he was awarded the Special Gold Medal by
National Geographic (　　　　)¹³ 1961. Later, his lifelong passion for environmental work would (　　　　)¹⁴ educate people on the necessity of
protecting the ocean (　　　　)¹⁵ aquatic life. For this he was honored
(　　　　)¹⁶ 1977 with the United Nations International Environment Prize.
Jacques Cousteau's life has inspired writers, filmmakers, and (　　　　)¹⁷
musicians. In 2010, Brad Matsen published *Jacques Cousteau: The Sea
King*. This was followed by the (　　　　)¹⁸ *The Odyssey* in 2016, which
shows his time (　　　　)¹⁹ the captain of the research boat Calypso.
When Cousteau (　　　　)²⁰ at the peak of his career, (　　　　)²¹ American musician John Denver used the research boat as the (　　　　)²² for a
piece on his (　　　　)²³ *Windsong*. Cousteau himself produced more than

50 books and 120 television documentaries. His first documentary series, *The Undersea World of Jacques Cousteau*, (   )²⁴ for ten years. His style of presentation (   )²⁵ these programs very popular, and a second documentary series, *The Cousteau Odyssey*, was (   )²⁶ for another five years. Thanks to the life (   )²⁷ work of Jacques Cousteau, we have a better understanding (   )²⁸ what is going on under (   )²⁹ waves.

MET 2022 追（2）日本語訳

問題英文の日本語訳を確認しよう。

彼は，長い間こう思っていた。イルカがエコーロケーション（音波によるナビゲーション）を使用しているのではないかと。それで，実験を試みることにした。クストーは，数度，ボートの方向を変えてみた。その結果，ボートは最適なコースをたどっていなかった。水中地図に照らしてみれば。イルカたちは，数分，クストーの後を追いかけてきたが，その後，元のコースに戻ってしまった。クストーはこれを見て，自分の予測，それは，イルカについての能力であるが，それが正しいことを確信した。人間によるエコーロケーションの使用はまだ比較的新しかったにもかかわらず。クストーの作品は，生涯を通じて，国際的に認められ続けた。彼は，カメラで捉える能力を持っていた。海面下の世界の美しさを。そして，その画像を一般の人々と共有した。多くの著書を通じて。この功績により，彼は 1961 年に，ナショナル・ジオグラフィック誌から特別金メダルを受賞した。その後，クストーは，生涯にわたって環境活動に情熱を持ち，これによって，人々は，教育されていった。海と水生生物を保護する必要性について。この功績により，1977 年に，国連国際環境賞を受賞した。ジャック・クストーの生涯は，作家，映画製作者，さらにはミュージシャンにまで影響を与えてきた。2010 年，ブラッド・マッツェンは，『ジャック・クストー 海の王』を出版した。続いて，2016 年に，映画『オデッセイ』が公開され，彼の時代を，調査船カリプソの船長として描いている。クストーが人生の絶頂期にあった時，アメリカの音楽家ジョン・デンバーは，その調査船を，アルバム『ウィンドソング』の中の一曲のタイトルとして使用した。クストー自身も，50 冊を超える書籍を出版し，テレビドキュメンタリーを 120 本制作した。彼の最初のドキュメンタリーシリーズ『ジャック・クストーの海底世界』は，10 年間にわたって放送された。彼の提示方法がよかったので，これらの番組は非常に人気になり，2 番目のドキュメンタリーシリーズ『クストーオデッセイ』は，さらに 5 年間放送された。ジャック・クストーの生涯と業績のおかげで，私たちは，より深く理解できるようになった。波の下で何が起こっているのかを。

MET 2022 追 (2) 解答

解答付き英文を見ながら，英語の音声をもう一度聞いてみよう。

He had long suspected that dolphins used echolocation (navigating (**with**)¹ sound waves), so he decided to (**try**)² an experiment. Cousteau changed direction by a few degrees so (**that**)³ the boat wasn't following the best course, according to (**his**)⁴ underwater maps. The dolphins followed for a few minutes, (**but**)⁵ then changed back to their original course. Seeing this, Cousteau confirmed (**his**)⁶ prediction about their ability, even though human use (**of**)⁷ echolocation was still relatively new. Throughout his life, Cousteau's (**work**)⁸ would continue to be recognized internationally. He had (**the**)⁹ ability to capture the beauty of the world (**below**)¹⁰ the surface of the ocean with cameras, (**and**)¹¹ he shared the images with ordinary people through his many publications. (**For**)¹² this he was awarded the Special Gold Medal by National Geographic (**in**)¹³ 1961. Later, his lifelong passion for environmental work would (**help**)¹⁴ educate people on the necessity of protecting the ocean (**and**)¹⁵ aquatic life. For this he was honored (**in**)¹⁶ 1977 with the United Nations International Environment Prize. Jacques Cousteau's life has inspired writers, filmmakers, and (**even**)¹⁷ musicians. In 2010, Brad Matsen published *Jacques Cousteau: The Sea King*. This was followed by the (**film**)¹⁸ *The Odyssey* in 2016, which shows his time (**as**)¹⁹ the captain of the research boat Calypso. When Cousteau (**was**)²⁰ at the peak of his career, (**the**)²¹ American musician John Denver used the research boat as the (**title**)²² for a piece on his (**album**)²³ *Windsong*. Cousteau himself produced more than 50 books and 120 television documentaries. His first documentary series, *The Undersea World of Jacques Cousteau*, (**ran**)²⁴ for ten years. His style of presentation (**made**)²⁵ these programs very popular, and a second documentary series, *The Cousteau Odyssey*, was (**aired**)²⁶ for another five years. Thanks to the life (**and**)²⁷ work of Jacques Cousteau, we have a better understanding (**of**)²⁸ what is going on under (**the**)²⁹ waves.

MET 2022 追 (3)

英語の音声を聞きながら，(　　) の中に，英単語を入れてください。

What are memories? Most people imagine them to (　　　　)[1] something like video recordings of events in our (　　　　)[2]. Whether it is a memory of love (　　　)[3] we treasure or something more like failure that (　　　)[4] fear, most of us believe our memories (　　　)[5] a permanent record of what happened. We may (　　　　)[6] that they get harder to recall as (　　　)[7] goes on, but we think (　　　)[8] remember the truth. Psychologists now tell us (　　　)[9] this is not the case. (　　　)[10] memories can change or even be changed. They (　　　)[11] move anywhere from slightly incorrect to absolutely false! According to well-known researcher Elizabeth Loftus, rather (　　　)[12] being a complete, correct, unchanging recording, "Memory works a little bit (　　　)[13] like a Wikipedia page." Anyone, including the original author, can (　　　)[14] the information. Serious research investigating "false memories" is relatively new. Scholars Hyman and Billings worked (　　　)[15] a group of college students. For this experiment, first, (　　　)[16] students' parents sent stories about some eventful episodes from their child's (　　　)[17] to the interviewers. Using this family information, they interviewed (　　　)[18] student twice. They mentioned some actual experiences from the person's childhood; (　　　)[19], for their experiment, they added a made-up (　　　)[20] about an eventful wedding, encouraging the student to believe the (　　　)[21] wedding had really happened. The following two sections contain actual conversations from the interviews of one student. (　　　)[22] interviewer, referring to the false event as (　　　)[23] the information came from the student's parent, goes (   )^{24} to say that while playing with friends (   )^{25} student caused an accident and the bride's parents got all (   )^{26}. The student is starting to believe that bumping into (   )^{27} table sounds familiar. As they finish, the student is (   )^{28} to think over the conversation they (   )^{29} before the next session.

MET 2022 追 (3) 日本語訳

問題英文の日本語訳を確認しよう。

記憶とは何だろう？ ほとんどの人は，こう想像するだろう。記憶とは，私たちの心の中の出来事をビデオで記録したようなものだと。それが私たちが大切にしている愛の記憶であっても，私たちが恐れている失敗に近いものであっても，私たちのほとんどは，こう信じている。自分の記憶は，起こったことの永続的な記録だと。記憶していることは，時間が経つほど，思い出しにくいということに同意するかもしれないが，私たちは，真実を覚えていると思っている。心理学者は，現在，実は，そうではないと言っている。私たちの記憶は変化する可能性があり，さらには変更される可能性がある。記憶は，わずかに間違っているものから完全に間違っているものまである。有名な研究者エリザベス・ロフタスによれば，完全で正確で不変の記録であるというよりは，「記憶は，もう少しウィキペディアのページのように機能する」ウィキペディアは，元の作成者を含む誰でも情報を編集できる。「偽りの記憶」を調査する本格的な研究は，比較的新しい。学者のハイマンとビリングスは，大学生のグループと共同で調査をした。この実験では，まず学生の保護者が，自分の子供の小さい頃の波瀾万丈なエピソードを面接官に送った。この家族情報を使用して，面接官は各学生に2回インタビューした。彼らは，その学生が幼少期から実際に経験したことを話した。しかし，実験として，波瀾万丈の結婚式についての作り話を加え，偽の結婚式が本当に起こったと学生に信じ込ませた。次の2つのセクションには，1人の学生へのインタビューからの実際の会話が含まれている。面接官は，あたかもその学生の親からの情報であるかのように，虚偽の出来事を話し，学生が友達と遊んでいた時に事件を起こし，その結果，新婦の両親がずぶ濡れになってしまったと続けた。学生は，テーブルにぶつかることはよくあることだと思い始めている。インタビューが終わると，その学生は，これまでに行った会話をもう一度振り返ってみるように求められる。次のセッションに入る前に。

MET 2022 追 (3) 解答

解答付き英文を見ながら，英語の音声をもう一度聞いてみよう。

What are memories? Most people imagine them to (**be**)[1] something like video recordings of events in our (**minds**)[2]. Whether it is a memory of love (**that**)[3] we treasure or something more like failure that (**we**)[4] fear, most of us believe our memories (**are**)[5] a permanent record of what happened. We may (**agree**)[6] that they get harder to recall as (**time**)[7] goes on, but we think (**we**)[8] remember the truth. Psychologists now tell us (**that**)[9] this is not the case. (**Our**)[10] memories can change or even be changed. They (**can**)[11] move anywhere from slightly incorrect to absolutely false! According to well-known researcher Elizabeth Loftus, rather (**than**)[12] being a complete, correct, unchanging recording, "Memory works a little bit (**more**)[13] like a Wikipedia page." Anyone, including the original author, can (**edit**)[14] the information. Serious research investigating "false memories" is relatively new. Scholars Hyman and Billings worked (**with**)[15] a group of college students. For this experiment, first, (**the**)[16] students' parents sent stories about some eventful episodes from their child's (**youth**)[17] to the interviewers. Using this family information, they interviewed (**each**)[18] student twice. They mentioned some actual experiences from the person's childhood; (**but**)[19], for their experiment, they added a made-up (**story**)[20] about an eventful wedding, encouraging the student to believe the (**fake**)[21] wedding had really happened. The following two sections contain actual conversations from the interviews of one student. (**The**)[22] interviewer, referring to the false event as (**if**)[23] the information came from the student's parent, goes (**on**)[24] to say that while playing with friends (**the**)[25] student caused an accident and the bride's parents got all (**wet**)[26]. The student is starting to believe that bumping into (**the**)[27] table sounds familiar. As they finish, the student is (**asked**)[28] to think over the conversation they (**had**)[29] before the next session.

英語の音声を聞きながら，（　　）の中に，英単語を入れてください。

The interviewer has just asked about (　　　　)[1] real events from the student's childhood and once (　　　　)[2] returns to the wedding discussed in the previous session. The student (　　　　)[3] on to describe the people he got (　　　　)[4]. The student has new images in mind (　　　　)[5] can tell this story as (　　　　)[6] it were an actual memory. This student then provides (　　　　)[7] information on the couple's clothing. The students participating in this experiment (　　　　)[8] to believe that the false experiences the interviewers planted (　　　　)[9] absolutely true. By the second interview some students thought everything previously discussed was (　　　　)[10] on information from their parents about real events. (　　　　)[11] suggests that, when talking about memories, word choice makes (　　　　)[12] big difference in responses. Certain words lead us (　　　　)[13] recall a situation differently. Because the interviewer mentioned an "eventful" wedding several times, the student started having (　　　　)[14] false memory of this wedding. Since the (　　　　)[15] of Sigmund Freud, called "the father of modern psychology," mental therapy has asked people (　　　　)[16] think back to their childhood to understand (　　　　)[17] problems. In the late 20th century, people believed that recalling old memories (　　　　)[18] a good way to heal (　　　　)[19] mind, so there were exercises and interviewing techniques encouraging patients (　　　　)[20] imagine various old family situations. Now, we realize that such activities (　　　　)[21] lead to false memories because our memories are affected (　　　　)[22] many factors. It is not just (　　　　)[23] we remember, but when we remember, where (   )²⁴ are when we remember, who is asking, (   )²⁵ how they are asking. We may, therefore, believe something (   )²⁶ comes from our imagination is actually true. Perhaps experts should (   )²⁷ researching whether there is such a thing (   )²⁸ "true memories."

MET 2022 追 (4) 日本語訳

問題英文の日本語訳を確認しよう。

面接官は，その学生の幼少期の実際の出来事について尋ねた。そして，再び，前回のセッションで話された結婚式の話に戻る。その学生は，続けて，自分がずぶ濡れにさせてしまった人々について説明する。その学生は，頭の中に新たなイメージを持ち，この物語がまるで実際の記憶であるかのように語る。次に，この学生は，このカップルの服装についてまで，あらたな情報を語り出す。この実験に参加した学生たちは，信じるようになっていた。面接官が植え付けた嘘の経験が，絶対的に正しいと。2回目のインタビューまでに，これまでに話し合われたことはすべて，実際の出来事について親からもたらされた情報に基づいていると考える学生もいた。これは，次のことを示唆している。記憶について話す時，言葉の選択によって，反応が大きく異なるということだ。特定の言葉によって，私たちは，ある状況をまったく別のもののように思い出すようになる。面接官が「波乱万丈な」結婚式について何度も語ったため，この学生は，この結婚式について誤った記憶を持つようになってしまった。ジークムント・フロイトは，「現代心理学の父」と呼ばれているが，その時代以来，メンタルセラピーでは，人々に子供時代を振り返るよう求めてきた。自分たちの問題を理解するために。20世紀後半，古い記憶を思い出すことは，心を癒すいい方法だと信じられていた。そのため，こんな練習や面接テクニックが存在した。それは，患者に古い家族のさまざまな状況を想像するよう促すようなものだ。現在，そのような活動は，誤った記憶につながる可能性があることが理解されてきた。私たちの記憶は，多くの要因に影響を受けるからだ。それは，私たちが何を覚えているかということだけではなく，いつ記憶するか，記憶する時にどこにいるか，誰が尋ねているか，そして，どのように尋ねているかなどだ。したがって，私たちは，こう信じてしまうかもしれない。自分の想像から来たものが実際に真実であると。おそらく専門家は，研究を始める必要があるだろう。「本当の記憶」というようものが存在するかどうかについて。

MET 2022 追（4）解答

解答付き英文を見ながら，英語の音声をもう一度聞いてみよう。

The interviewer has just asked about (**some**)[1] real events from the student's childhood and once (**again**)[2] returns to the wedding discussed in the previous session. The student (**goes**)[3] on to describe the people he got (**wet**)[4]. The student has new images in mind (**and**)[5] can tell this story as (**if**)[6] it were an actual memory. This student then provides (**more**)[7] information on the couple's clothing. The students participating in this experiment (**came**)[8] to believe that the false experiences the interviewers planted (**were**)[9] absolutely true. By the second interview some students thought everything previously discussed was (**based**)[10] on information from their parents about real events. (**This**)[11] suggests that, when talking about memories, word choice makes (**a**)[12] big difference in responses. Certain words lead us (**to**)[13] recall a situation differently. Because the interviewer mentioned an "eventful" wedding several times, the student started having (**a**)[14] false memory of this wedding. Since the (**time**)[15] of Sigmund Freud, called "the father of modern psychology," mental therapy has asked people (**to**)[16] think back to their childhood to understand (**their**)[17] problems. In the late 20th century, people believed that recalling old memories (**was**)[18] a good way to heal (**the**)[19] mind, so there were exercises and interviewing techniques encouraging patients (**to**)[20] imagine various old family situations. Now, we realize that such activities (**may**)[21] lead to false memories because our memories are affected (**by**)[22] many factors. It is not just (**what**)[23] we remember, but when we remember, where (**we**)[24] are when we remember, who is asking, (**and**)[25] how they are asking. We may, therefore, believe something (**that**)[26] comes from our imagination is actually true. Perhaps experts should (**start**)[27] researching whether there is such a thing (**as**)[28] "true memories."

MET 2022 追 (5)

英語の音声を聞きながら，（　　）の中に，英単語を入れてください。

Since ancient times, people have measured things. Measuring helps humans say (　　　　)[1] long, far, big, or heavy something (　　　　)[2] with some kind of accuracy. While weight (　　　　)[3] volume are important for the exchange of food, (　　　　)[4] can be argued that one of the (　　　　)[5] useful measurements is length because it is needed to calculate area, (　　　　)[6] helps in the exchange, protection, and taxation of property. Measuring systems (　　　　)[7] often be based on or related (　　　　)[8] the human body. One of the earliest (　　　　)[9] measuring systems was the cubit, which was created around the 3rd millennium BC (　　　　)[10] Egypt and Mesopotamia. One cubit was the length of a man's forearm (　　　　)[11] the elbow to the tip (　　　　)[12] the middle finger, which according to one royal standard was 524 millimeters (mm). (　　　　)[13] addition, the old Roman foot (296 mm), which probably came from (　　　　)[14] Egyptians, was based on a human (　　　　)[15]. A unit of measurement known as (　　　　)[16] yard probably originated in Britain after the Roman occupation and it (　　　　)[17] said to be based on (　　　　)[18] double cubit. Whatever its origin, there were several different yards in use (　　　　)[19] Britain. Each one was a different length until the 12th century (　　　　)[20] the yard was standardized as the length from King Henry I's (　　　　)[21] to his thumb on his outstretched (　　　　)[22]. But it was not until (　　　　)[23] 14th century that official documents described the yard as being divided into three (　　　　)[24] parts—three feet— with one foot consisting of 12 inches. While this description helped standardize (   )^25 inch and foot, it wasn't until the late 15th century, (   )^26 King Henry VII distributed official metal samples of feet and yards, that people knew (   )^27 certain their true length. Over the years, (   )^28 number of small adjustments were made until (   )^29 International Yard and Pound Agreement of 1959 finally defined the standard inch, foot, and yard as 25.4 mm, 304.8 mm, and 914.4 mm respectively.

MET 2022 追（5）日本語訳

問題英文の日本語訳を確認しよう。

太古の昔から，人々は物を測ってきた。測定は，こんなことに役立つ。人が，何かの長さ，距離，大きさ，重さをある種の正確さで語るのに。食物の交換には重量と体積が重要であるが，最も有用な測定値の1つは長さであると言える。というのも，長さは，面積の計算に必要となるからだ。面積は，財産の交換，保護，課税に役立つのだ。測定システムは，多くの場合，人体に基づいているか，人体に関連している。これまで知られている最も初期の測定システムの1つは，キュビットで，紀元前3000年頃にエジプトとメソポタミアで作成された。1キュビットは，男性の前腕部の長さで，肘から中指の先までの長さである。ある王室基準によれば，これは524ミリメートル（mm）だった。さらに，古代ローマの単位フット（296 mm）は，おそらくエジプト人から来たもので，人間の足をベースにしている。ヤードとして知られる測定単位は，おそらくローマによる占領後にイギリスで誕生し，2キュビットに基づいていると言われている。その起源が何であれ，イギリスでは異なるヤードがいくつか使用されていた。12世紀までヤードのそれぞれの長さは異なっていた。その頃，ヤードという単位は，ヘンリー1世の鼻から伸ばした腕の親指までの長さとして標準化された。しかし，14世紀になってから，公式文書に，次のことが記載された。ヤードは，3つの等しい部分（3フィート）に分割され，その1フィートは，12インチであった。この記述によって，インチとフィートがうまい具合に標準化されたが，15世紀後半になってようやく，ヘンリー7世がフィートとヤードの公式金属サンプルを配布し，その結果，人々がフィートとヤードの実際の長さを確実に知るようになった。長年にわたって小さな調整が何度も行われ，1959年の国際ヤード・ポンド協定で，最終的に標準のインチ，フィート，ヤードがそれぞれ25.4 mm，304.8 mm，914.4 mmと定義された。

MET 2022 追（5）解答

解答付き英文を見ながら，英語の音声をもう一度聞いてみよう。

Since ancient times, people have measured things. Measuring helps humans say (**how**)[1] long, far, big, or heavy something (**is**)[2] with some kind of accuracy. While weight (**and**)[3] volume are important for the exchange of food, (**it**)[4] can be argued that one of the (**most**)[5] useful measurements is length because it is needed to calculate area, (**which**)[6] helps in the exchange, protection, and taxation of property. Measuring systems (**would**)[7] often be based on or related (**to**)[8] the human body. One of the earliest (**known**)[9] measuring systems was the cubit, which was created around the 3rd millennium BC (**in**)[10] Egypt and Mesopotamia. One cubit was the length of a man's forearm (**from**)[11] the elbow to the tip (**of**)[12] the middle finger, which according to one royal standard was 524 millimeters (mm). (**In**)[13] addition, the old Roman foot (296 mm), which probably came from (**the**)[14] Egyptians, was based on a human (**foot**)[15]. A unit of measurement known as (**the**)[16] yard probably originated in Britain after the Roman occupation and it (**is**)[17] said to be based on (**the**)[18] double cubit. Whatever its origin, there were several different yards in use (**in**)[19] Britain. Each one was a different length until the 12th century (**when**)[20] the yard was standardized as the length from King Henry I's (**nose**)[21] to his thumb on his outstretched (**arm**)[22]. But it was not until (**the**)[23] 14th century that official documents described the yard as being divided into three (**equal**)[24] parts—three feet—with one foot consisting of 12 inches. While this description helped standardize (**the**)[25] inch and foot, it wasn't until the late 15th century, (**when**)[26] King Henry VII distributed official metal samples of feet and yards, that people knew (**for**)[27] certain their true length. Over the years, (**a**)[28] number of small adjustments were made until (**the**)[29] International Yard and Pound Agreement of 1959 finally defined the standard inch, foot, and yard as 25.4 mm, 304.8 mm, and 914.4 mm respectively.

英語の音声を聞きながら，（　　）の中に，英単語を入れてください。

The use of the human (　　　　)[1] as a standard from which to develop (　　　　)[2] measuring system was not unique to western cultures. The traditional Chinese unit (　　　　)[3] length called *chi*—now one-third of a meter—was originally defined as (　　　　)[4] length from the tip of the (　　　　)[5] to the outstretched tip of the middle finger, (　　　　)[6] was around 200 mm. However, over the years it increased (　　　　)[7] length and became known as the Chinese foot. Interestingly, the Japanese *shaku*, (　　　　)[8] was based on the *chi*, is almost (　　　　)[9] same as one standard foot. It is only 1.8 mm shorter. (　　　　)[10] connection between the human body and measurement can (　　　　)[11] be found in sailing. The fathom (6 feet), the best-known (　　　　)[12] for measuring the depth of the (　　　　)[13] in the English-speaking world, was historically an ancient Greek measurement. (　　　　)[14] was not a very accurate measurement as (　　　　)[15] was based on the length of (　　　　)[16] a sailor could extend from open arm (　　　　)[17] open arm. Like many other British (　　　　)[18] American units, it was also standardized in 1959. (　　　　)[19] metric system, first described in 1668 and officially adopted by the French government in 1799, (　　　　)[20] now become the dominant measuring system worldwide. This system has slowly been adopted (　　　　)[21] many countries as either their standard measuring system or as (　　　　)[22] alternative to their traditional system. While the metric system is mainly (　　　　)[23] by the scientific, medical, and industrial professions, traditional commercial activities still continue to (　　　　)[24] local traditional measuring systems. For example, in Japan, window widths are measured in *ken* (6 *shaku*). (　　　　)[25], an understanding of the relationship between different measures was only something traders (　　　　)[26] tax officials needed to know. However, now that international online shopping (　　　　)[27] spread around the world, we all need (　　　　)[28] know a little about other countries' measuring systems so (　　　　)[29] we know how much, or (　　　　)[30] little, of something we are buying.

MET 2022 追 (6) 日本語訳

問題英文の日本語訳を確認しよう。

人体を基準として，測定システムを開発することは，西洋文化に特有のものではなかった。中国の伝統的な長さの単位である「チー」（現在は 1 メートルの 3 分の 1）は，もともとは，親指の先端から，指を広げた状態での中指の先端までの長さとして定義されており，約 200 mm だった。しかし，長い年月が経つにつれ，それはだんだん長くなり，中国の「フィート」として知られるようになった。おもしろいことに，日本の「尺」は，「チー」を基準にしているが，標準的な 1 フィートとほぼ同じである。わずか 1.8 mm 短いだけだ。人体と測定の関係はセーリングにも見られる。ファゾム（6 フィート）は，英語圏における海の深さを測る単位として最もよく知られているが，歴史的には古代ギリシャの単位だった。これは，あまり正確な単位ではなかった。というのも，船乗りが，両腕を広げた時の，腕から腕までロープを伸ばした，その長さに基づいていたからである。他の多くのイギリスやアメリカの単位と同様に，これも 1959 年に標準化された。メートル法は，1668 年に初めて記述され，1799 年にフランス政府によって正式に採用され，現在では世界中で主流の測定システムとなっている。このシステムは，徐々に採用されてきた。多くの国で，標準測定システムとして。あるいは，従来のシステムの代替システムとして。メートル法は主に，科学，医療，産業の専門家によって使用されているが，伝統的な商業活動では，依然として，地域の伝統的な測定システムが使用され続けている。例えば，日本では，戸の幅は，「間（6 尺）」で測定される。かつては，さまざまな指標間の関係を理解することは，商人と税務職員のみが知ってけばよいことだった。しかし，今や，国際的なオンラインショッピングが世界中に普及し，私たちは皆，他国の測定システムについて，少しは知る必要がある。自分が購入している商品がどれだけの量であるかを知るために。

MET 2022 追 (6) 解答

解答付き英文を見ながら，英語の音声をもう一度聞いてみよう。

The use of the human (**body**)[1] as a standard from which to develop (**a**)[2] measuring system was not unique to western cultures. The traditional Chinese unit (**of**)[3] length called *chi*—now one-third of a meter—was originally defined as (**the**)[4] length from the tip of the (**thumb**)[5] to the out-stretched tip of the middle finger, (**which**)[6] was around 200 mm. However, over the years it increased (**in**)[7] length and became known as the Chinese foot. Interestingly, the Japanese *shaku*, (**which**)[8] was based on the *chi*, is almost (**the**)[9] same as one standard foot. It is only 1.8 mm shorter. (**The**)[10] connection between the human body and measurement can (**also**)[11] be found in sailing. The fathom (6 feet), the best-known (**unit**)[12] for measuring the depth of the (**sea**)[13] in the English-speaking world, was historically an ancient Greek measurement. (**It**)[14] was not a very accurate measurement as (**it**)[15] was based on the length of (**rope**)[16] a sailor could extend from open arm (**to**)[17] open arm. Like many other British (**and**)[18] American units, it was also standardized in 1959. (**The**)[19] metric system, first described in 1668 and officially adopted by the French government in 1799, (**has**)[20] now become the dominant measuring system worldwide. This system has slowly been adopted (**by**)[21] many countries as either their standard measuring system or as (**an**)[22] alternative to their traditional system. While the metric system is mainly (**used**)[23] by the scientific, medical, and industrial professions, traditional commercial activities still continue to (**use**)[24] local traditional measuring systems. For example, in Japan, window widths are measured in *ken* (6 *shaku*). (**Once**)[25], an understanding of the relationship between different measures was only something traders (**and**)[26] tax officials needed to know. However, now that international online shopping (**has**)[27] spread around the world, we all need (**to**)[28] know a little about other countries' measuring systems so (**that**)[29] we know how much, or (**how**)[30] little, of something we are buying.

MET 2023 追（1）

英語の音声を聞きながら，（　　）の中に，英単語を入れてください。

Lucy smiled in anticipation. In a moment she (　　　　)¹ walk onto the stage (　　　　)² receive her prize from the (　　　　)³ and the judges of the drawing contest. (　　　　)⁴ microphone screeched and then came the mayor's announcement. "(　　　　)⁵ the winner of the drawing contest is … Robert McGinnis! Congratulations!" Lucy (　　　　)⁶ up, still smiling. Then, her (　　　　)⁷ blazing red with embarrassment, abruptly sat down (　　　　)⁸. What? There must be (　　　　)⁹ mistake! But the boy named Robert McGinnis (　　　　)¹⁰ already on the stage, shaking hands (　　　　)¹¹ the mayor and accepting the (　　　　)¹². She glanced at her parents, her (　　　　)¹³ filled with tears of disappointment. They (　　　　)¹⁴ expected her to do well, especially (　　　　)¹⁵ father. "Oh Daddy, I'm sorry I didn't win," she whispered. Lucy (　　　　)¹⁶ enjoyed drawing since she was a little (　　　　)¹⁷. She did her first drawing of (　　　　)¹⁸ father when she was in kindergarten. Although (　　　　)¹⁹ was only a child's drawing, it really looked (　　　　)²⁰ him. He was de-lighted, and, (　　　　)²¹ that day, Lucy spent many (　　　　)²² hours drawing pictures to give to Mommy (　　　　)²³ Daddy. As she got older, (　　　　)²⁴ parents continued to encourage her. Her mother, a (　　　　)²⁵ translator, was happy that her daughter (　　　　)²⁶ doing something creative. Her father bought her art (　　　　)²⁷. He was no artist himself, but sometimes (　　　　)²⁸ her advice, suggesting that she look (　　　　)²⁹ carefully at what she was drawing (　　　　)³⁰ copy as accurately as possible. Lucy tried (　　　　)³¹, wanting to improve her technique and please her father. (   )^{32} had been Lucy's idea to (   )^{33} the town drawing contest. She thought that (   )^{34} she won, her artistic ability would (   )^{35} recognized. She practiced every evening after school. She (   )^{36} spent all her weekends working quietly on (   )^{37} drawings, copying her subjects as carefully as she (   )^{38}. Her failure to do well (   )^{39} as a great shock. (   )^{40} had worked so hard and (   )^{41} parents had been so sup-portive.

MET 2023 追（1）日本語訳

問題英文の日本語訳を確認しよう。

ルーシーは期待して微笑んだ。今すぐにでも，彼女はステージに上がり，市長と写生コンテストの審査員から賞品を受け取ろうとした。マイクがキーンと鳴って，市長のアナウンスが流れた。「さあ，写生コンテストの優勝者は … ロバート・マクギニスです！ おめでとう！」ルーシーは立ち上がって，まだ微笑んでいた。その直後，彼女は恥ずかしさで顔を真っ赤にして，突然また座り直した。何ですって？ 何かが間違ってるに違いないわ！ しかし，ロバート・マクギニスという名前の少年はすでにステージに上がり，市長と握手して賞品を受け取っていた。彼女は両親をちらっと見たが，その目には失望の涙があふれていた。両親は，彼女がうまくいくことを期待していた。特に父親が。「ああ，パパ，勝てなくてごめんなさい」と彼女はささやいた。ルーシーは，幼い頃から絵を描くのが好きだった。彼女が初めて父親の絵を描いたのは，幼稚園の時だった。子供の絵なのに本当にそっくりだった。彼は大喜びし，その日からルーシーは，ずっと幸せな時間を過ごした。パパとママにプレゼントする絵を描いて。彼女が成長しても，両親は彼女を励まし続けた。母親は，翻訳者として多忙であったが，娘が何か創造的なことをしていることを喜んでいた。父親は，彼女に絵画集を買い与えた。彼自身はアーティストではなかったが，時々彼女にアドバイスを与え，こんな提案もした。描いているものを注意深く見て，できるだけ正確に模倣してみようと。ルーシーは，一所懸命努力した。そして，自分の技術を向上させて，父親を喜ばせたかった。町の絵のコンテストに参加しようと言い出したのは，ルーシーだった。彼女は，勝てば自分の芸術的才能が認められると思った。彼女は毎晩放課後に練習した。彼女はまた，週末をずっと静かに絵の制作に費やし，できるだけ注意深く対象を模倣した。彼女がコンテストで思うような結果が得られなかったことは，大きなショックだった。彼女は一所懸命頑張り，そして両親はとても協力的でいてくれたのに。

MET 2023 追（1）解答

解答付き英文を見ながら，英語の音声をもう一度聞いてみよう。

Lucy smiled in anticipation. In a moment she（**would**）[1] walk onto the stage（**and**）[2] receive her prize from the（**mayor**）[3] and the judges of the drawing contest.（**The**）[4] microphone screeched and then came the mayor's announcement. "（**And**）[5] the winner of the drawing contest is... Robert McGinnis! Congratulations!" Lucy（**stood**）[6] up, still smiling. Then, her（**face**）[7] blazing red with embarrassment, abruptly sat down（**again**）[8]. What? There must be（**a**）[9] mistake! But the boy named Robert McGinnis（**was**）[10] already on the stage, shaking hands（**with**）[11] the mayor and accepting the（**prize**）[12]. She glanced at her parents, her（**eyes**）[13] filled with tears of disappointment. They（**had**）[14] expected her to do well, especially（**her**）[15] father. "Oh Daddy, I'm sorry I didn't win," she whispered. Lucy（**had**）[16] enjoyed drawing since she was a little（**girl**）[17]. She did her first drawing of（**her**）[18] father when she was in kindergarten. Although（**it**）[19] was only a child's drawing, it really looked（**like**）[20] him. He was delighted, and,（**from**）[21] that day, Lucy spent many（**happy**）[22] hours drawing pictures to give to Mommy（**and**）[23] Daddy. As she got older,（**her**）[24] parents continued to encourage her. Her mother, a（**busy**）[25] translator, was happy that her daughter（**was**）[26] doing something creative. Her father bought her art（**books**）[27]. He was no artist himself, but sometimes（**gave**）[28] her advice, suggesting that she look（**very**）[29] carefully at what she was drawing（**and**）[30] copy as accurately as possible. Lucy tried（**hard**）[31], wanting to improve her technique and please her father.（**It**）[32] had been Lucy's idea to（**enter**）[33] the town drawing contest. She thought that（**if**）[34] she won, her artistic ability would（**be**）[35] recognized. She practiced every evening after school. She（**also**）[36] spent all her weekends working quietly on（**her**）[37] drawings, copying her subjects as carefully as she（**could**）[38]. Her failure to do well（**came**）[39] as a great shock.（**She**）[40] had worked so hard and（**her**）[41] parents had been so supportive.

英語の音声を聞きながら, ( ) の中に, 英単語を入れてください。

Her father, however, was puzzled. Why did Lucy apologize ( )[1] the end of the contest? ( )[2] was no need to ( )[3] so. Later, Lucy asked him ( )[4] she had failed to win ( )[5] competition. He answered sympathetically, "To me, your drawing ( )[6] perfect." Then he smiled, and added, "( )[7] perhaps you should talk to your mother. ( )[8] understands art better than I do." ( )[9] mother was thoughtful.   She wanted to give Lucy advice without damaging ( )[10] daughter's self-esteem.   "Your drawing was good," she ( )[11] her, "but I think ( )[12] lacked something. I think you only ( )[13] what you could see. ( )[14] I translate a novel, I ( )[15] to capture not only the meaning, ( )[16] also the spirit of the original. ( )[17] do that, I need ( )[18] consider the meaning behind the words. Perhaps drawing is ( )[19] same; you need to ( )[20] under the surface." Lucy continued to draw, ( )[21] her art left her feeling unsatisfied. ( )[22] couldn't understand what her mother meant.   What ( )[23] wrong with drawing what she ( )[24] see? What else could ( )[25] do? Around this time, Lucy became friends with ( )[26] girl called Cathy. They became close friends and Lucy ( )[27] to appreciate her for her kindness ( )[28] humorous personality. Cathy often made Lucy laugh, telling jokes, saying ridiculous things, ( )[29] making funny faces. One afternoon, Cathy had such ( )[30] funny expression on her face ( )[31] Lucy felt she had to ( )[32] it. "Hold that pose!"

(   )³³ told Cathy, laughing. She drew quickly, enjoying her friend's expression (   )³⁴ much that she didn't really think (   )³⁵ what she was doing. (   )³⁶ Lucy entered art college three years later, she (   )³⁷ had that sketch. It had caught Cathy exactly, (   )³⁸ only her odd expression but (   )³⁹ her friend's kindness and her sense (   )⁴⁰ humor—the things that are (   )⁴¹ under the sur-face.

MET 2023 追（2）日本語訳

問題英文の日本語訳を確認しよう。

しかし，彼女の父親は困惑していた。なぜルーシーはコンテストの終わりに謝ってきたのだろう？ そうする必要は，まったくなかったのに。その後，ルーシーは，なぜコンテストに勝てなかったのかと彼に尋ねてきた。彼は同情的にこう答えた。「お父さんにとっては，ルーシーの絵は完璧だったよ」そして，彼は微笑んで，こう付け加えた。「でも，お母さんに相談したほうがいいかもしれないね。お母さんは，お父さんよりも，芸術のことがよくわかっているから」母親は思慮深い人だった。彼女は娘の自尊心を傷つけることなく，ルーシーにアドバイスを与えたかったのだ。「ルーシーの絵は，上手だったよ」と彼女は言った。「しかし，何かが欠けていたような気がする。目に見えるものだけを描いたような。私が小説を翻訳する時は，意味だけでなく，原文が言わんとしていることも捉える必要があるの。そのためには，言葉の背後にある意味を考える必要があるの。おそらく絵を描くことも同じじゃないかなあ。目に見えているものの後ろに何があるかを見る必要があるんじゃないかな」ルーシーは絵を描き続けたが，自分の絵には満足できなかった。彼女には母親が何を言いたかったか理解できなかった。目に見えるものを描いて，何が問題なの？ 他に何ができるって言うの？ この頃，ルーシーはキャシーという女の子と友達になった。二人は親しくなり，ルーシーは彼女の優しさとユーモアがある人柄に感謝するようになった。キャシーは，よくルーシーを笑わせた。ジョークを言ったり，ばかばかしいことを言ったり，変な顔をしたりして。ある午後，キャシーがとてもおかしな表情をしていたので，ルーシーはそれを描かなきゃと感じた。「そのポーズのままで！」彼女は，キャシーに笑いながら言った。彼女は，素早く絵を描いた。友人の表情を楽しみながら，自分が何をしているのかあまり考えずに。3年後，ルーシーが美術大学に入学した時，彼女はまだそのスケッチを持っていた。それは，正確に捉えていた。キャシーの奇妙な表情だけでなく，彼女の友人としての優しさやユーモアのセンスも。つまり，目に見えているものの後ろにある何かを。

MET 2023 追（2）解答

解答付き英文を見ながら，英語の音声をもう一度聞いてみよう。

Her father, however, was puzzled. Why did Lucy apologize（**at**）[1] the end of the contest?（**There**）[2] was no need to（**do**）[3] so. Later, Lucy asked him（**why**）[4] she had failed to win（**the**）[5] competition. He answered sympathetically, "To me, your drawing（**was**）[6] perfect." Then he smiled, and added, "（**But**）[7] perhaps you should talk to your mother.（**She**）[8] understands art better than I do."（**Her**）[9] mother was thoughtful. She wanted to give Lucy advice without damaging（**her**）[10] daughter's self-esteem. "Your drawing was good," she（**told**）[11] her, "but I think（**it**）[12] lacked something. I think you only（**drew**）[13] what you could see.（**When**）[14] I translate a novel, I（**need**）[15] to capture not only the meaning,（**but**）[16] also the spirit of the original.（**To**）[17] do that, I need（**to**）[18] consider the meaning behind the words. Perhaps drawing is（**the**）[19] same; you need to（**look**）[20] under the surface." Lucy continued to draw,（**but**）[21] her art left her feeling unsatisfied.（**She**）[22] couldn't understand what her mother meant. What（**was**）[23] wrong with drawing what she（**could**）[24] see? What else could（**she**）[25] do? Around this time, Lucy became friends with（**a**）[26] girl called Cathy. They became close friends and Lucy（**grew**）[27] to appreciate her for her kindness（**and**）[28] humorous personality. Cathy often made Lucy laugh, telling jokes, saying ridiculous things,（**and**）[29] making funny faces. One afternoon, Cathy had such（**a**）[30] funny expression on her face（**that**）[31] Lucy felt she had to（**draw**）[32] it. "Hold that pose!"（**she**）[33] told Cathy, laughing. She drew quickly, enjoying her friend's expression（**so**）[34] much that she didn't really think（**about**）[35] what she was doing.（**When**）[36] Lucy entered art college three years later, she（**still**）[37] had that sketch. It had caught Cathy exactly,（**not**）[38] only her odd expression but（**also**）[39] her friend's kindness and her sense（**of**）[40] humor—the things that are（**found**）[41] under the surface.

MET 2023 追 (3)

英語の音声を聞きながら，（　）の中に，英単語を入れてください。

The mysteries of the deep (　　　　)[1] sea have fascinated ocean-watchers for millennia. Aquatic beings, however, cannot easily get (　　　　)[2] us. What if we (　　　　)[3] to them? Despite what you (　　　　)[4] expect, certain ocean animals will come right (　　　　)[5] to you. Dan McSweeney, a Hawaii-based underwater research photographer, tells (　　　　)[6] fascinating story. While he was studying whales underwater, one (　　　　)[7] charging at him. Whales are huge, (　　　　)[8] he was worried. The whale stopped, opened (　　　　)[9] mouth, and "passed" him some (　　　　)[10]. He accepted the gift. McSweeney believes that because (　　　　)[11] the air bubbles coming from his (　　　　)[12], the whale recognized him as (　　　　)[13] similar animal and offered the *sashimi*. Later, the (　　　　)[14] came back, and McSweeney returned the (　　　　)[15]. Friendly interactions with dolphins or whales are possible, but (　　　　)[16] about octopuses? Science fiction sometimes describes aliens as looking like octopuses, so (　　　　)[17] animal group "cephalopods," which means "head-feet," may (　　　　)[18] perceived as being distant from humans. Yet, (　　　　)[19] you learn more about (　　　　)[20], you might be convinced there (　　　　)[21] the possibility of interaction. Octopuses have long tentacles (arms/legs) extending (　　　　)[22] soft round bodies. Besides touch and motion, (　　　　)[23] tentacle experiences smell and taste and (　　　　)[24] sucking disks, called suckers, that grab and manipulate things. (　　　　)[25] eyes, like two independent cameras, can move 80° (　　　　)[26] focus on two different things at once. UC Berkeley researcher,

Alexander Stubbs, confirms (   )^{27} while octopuses sense light and (   )^{28} differently from humans, they do recognize color changes. (   )^{29} features might indicate that they are intelligent enough (   )^{30} interact with us. In fact, (   )^{31} article in *Everyday Mysteries* begins: "Question. Can an octopus get (   )^{32} know you? Answer. Yes." Octopuses are known (   )^{33} "return your gaze" when you (   )^{34} at them. They may (   )^{35} remember you. This notion was tested by Roland C. Anderson (   )^{36} his colleagues, who conducted experiments with two similar-looking people wearing the (   )^{37} uniforms.

MET 2023 追（3）日本語訳

問題英文の日本語訳を確認しよう。

紺碧の海の神秘に，海洋観察者たちは，何千年もの間，魅了されてきた。しかしながら，水生生物は，人間にはなかなか近づいてこない。では，人間が，彼らのところに行ったらどうなるだろうか？ 予想とは裏腹に，海洋動物の中には，人間のところに近づいてくるものもある。ダン・マクスウィーニーは，ハワイを拠点とする水中調査写真家であるが，わくわくさせるような話を語ってくれる。彼が水中でクジラを研究していると，一頭のクジラが彼に向かって突進してきた。クジラは大きいので，マクスウィーニーは心配していた。ところが，クジラは立ち止まり，口を開け，彼にマグロを「手渡した」。彼は，贈り物を受け取った。マクスウィーニーは，こんなことが起きたのではないかと考えている。酸素ボンベから出る泡のせいで，クジラが彼を自分と似た動物として認識し，刺身を手渡してくれたのではないかと。その後，そのクジラは戻ってきて，マクスウィーニーはその餌をクジラに返した。イルカやクジラと友好的に交流することは可能であるが，タコはどうだろうか？ SF では，宇宙人の姿をタコのように描くことがあるため，この動物グループは，「頭足類」（「頭と足」を意味する）と呼ばれるが，人間とは遠い存在として認識されているかもしれない。しかしながら，タコについて詳しく学べば，タコと交流できる可能性があると確信するかもしれない。タコは，長い触手（腕 / 脚）を持っていて，それは，柔らかい丸い体から伸びている。それぞれの触手は，触ったり，動いたりするだけでなく，匂いや味を感じ，吸い取るような円盤を持っている。これは，吸盤と呼ばれ，物を掴んだり，操作したりする。タコの目は，2 台の独立したカメラのように，80° 移動し，一度に 2 つの異なるものに焦点を合わせることができる。カリフォルニア大学バークレー校の研究者，アレクサンダー・スタッブスは，次のことを確認している。タコは，光と色の感覚が人間とは異なるものの，色の変化は認識しているということだ。これらの特徴は，次のことを示している可能性がある。タコは，十分知性を持っており，人間と対話することができるという可能性だ。もっと言うと，『Everyday Mysteries』の記事は次のように始まる。「質問。タコはあなたのことが，あなただとわかるか？ 答え。わかります」タコは，「視線を返す」ことで知られている。見つめられると。タコは，あなたのことを覚えてさえいるかもしれない。この概念は，ローランド C. アンダーソンとその同僚によってテストされた。彼らは，実験を行った。見た目がそっくりの，同じ制服を着た 2 人を使って。

MET 2023 追 (3) 解答

解答付き英文を見ながら，英語の音声をもう一度聞いてみよう。

The mysteries of the deep (**blue**)[1] sea have fascinated ocean-watchers for millennia. Aquatic beings, however, cannot easily get (**to**)[2] us. What if we (**go**)[3] to them? Despite what you (**may**)[4] expect, certain ocean animals will come right (**up**)[5] to you. Dan McSweeney, a Hawaii-based underwater research photographer, tells (**a**)[6] fascinating story. While he was studying whales underwater, one (**came**)[7] charging at him. Whales are huge, (**so**)[8] he was worried. The whale stopped, opened (**its**)[9] mouth, and "passed" him some (**tuna**)[10]. He accepted the gift. McSweeney believes that because (**of**)[11] the air bubbles coming from his (**tank**)[12], the whale recognized him as (**a**)[13] similar animal and offered the *sashimi*. Later, the (**whale**)[14] came back, and McSweeney returned the (**food**)[15]. Friendly interactions with dolphins or whales are possible, but (**how**)[16] about octopuses? Science fiction sometimes describes aliens as looking like octopuses, so (**this**)[17] animal group "cephalopods," which means "head-feet," may (**be**)[18] perceived as being distant from humans. Yet, (**if**)[19] you learn more about (**them**)[20], you might be convinced there (**is**)[21] the possibility of interaction. Octopuses have long tentacles (arms/legs) extending (**from**)[22] soft round bodies. Besides touch and motion, (**each**)[23] tentacle experiences smell and taste and (**has**)[24] sucking disks, called suckers, that grab and manipulate things. (**Their**)[25] eyes, like two independent cameras, can move 80° (**and**)[26] focus on two different things at once. UC Berkeley researcher, Alexander Stubbs, confirms (**that**)[27] while octopuses sense light and (**color**)[28] differently from humans, they do recognize color changes. (**These**)[29] features might indicate that they are intelligent enough (**to**)[30] interact with us. In fact, (**an**)[31] article in *Everyday Mysteries* begins: "Question. Can an octopus get (**to**)[32] know you? Answer. Yes." Octopuses are known (**to**)[33] "return your gaze" when you (**look**)[34] at them. They may (**even**)[35] remember you. This notion was tested by Roland C. Anderson (**and**)[36] his colleagues, who conducted experiments with two similar-looking people wearing the (**same**)[37] uniforms.

MET 2023 追（4）

英語の音声を聞きながら，（　　）の中に，英単語を入れてください。

The friendly person, who had fed (　　　　)[1] socialized with them, got a completely different reaction (　　　　)[2] the cephalopods than the other person (　　　　)[3] had not. When taken (　　　　)[4] their natural habitat, octopuses can be mischievous, so (　　　　)[5] out. They can push (　　　　)[6] lids off their tanks, escape, (　　　　)[7] go for a walk. Scientists sometimes (　　　　)[8] surprise visits. A paper from the Naples Zoological Station, written (　　　　)[9] 1959, talks about trying to teach three octopuses (　　　　)[10] pull a lever down (　　　　)[11] food. Two of them, Albert and Bertram, cooperated (　　　　)[12] the experiment, but Charles, a clever cephalopod, refused to (　　　　)[13] so. He shot water (　　　　)[14] the scientists and ended the experiment (　　　　)[15] breaking the equipment. If you are interested (　　　　)[16] seeing their natural behavior and interactions, getting into the (　　　　)[17] and having them come to (　　　　)[18] might work better. They may (　　　　)[19] raise a tentacle to motion you (　　　　)[20]. Around 2007, Peter Godfrey-Smith, a philosophy professor teaching at Harvard University, was home (　　　　)[21] vacation in Sydney, Australia. Exploring in the ocean, (　　　　)[22] came across a giant cephalopod. Godfrey-Smith was (　　　　)[23] impressed by the behavior he witnessed that (　　　　)[24] started developing philosophy theories based on his observations. Determined to (　　　　)[25] out what humans could learn (　　　　)[26] cephalopods, Godfrey-Smith let them guide him. (　　　　)[27] one ocean trip, another cephalopod took Godfrey-Smith's colleague by (　　　　)[28] hand on a 10-minute tour

(   )²⁹ the octopus's home, "as if (   )³⁰ were being led across the (   )³¹ floor by a very (   )³², eightlegged child!" How can you get (   )³³ creatures to come to you (   )³⁴ you don't swim? The Kahn family has solved (   )³⁵ with "Coral World" in Eilat, Israel. The lowest floor (   )³⁶ the building is actually con-structed in the Red Sea, creating (   )³⁷ "human display." Rather than the sea-life performances at many aquariums, (   )³⁸ find yourself in a "people tank," where curious (   )³⁹ and sea creatures, swimming freely in the (   )⁴⁰, come to look at (   )⁴¹. To make a good impression, (   )⁴² may want to wear (   )⁴³ clothes.

MET 2023 追（4）日本語訳

問題英文の日本語訳を確認しよう。

一方の人は，友好的で，餌をあげてタコと交流した。この頭足類の動物は，こんな反応を示した。それは，もう一方の人，その人はタコに対して友好的ではなかったのだが，その人に示した反応とは，まったく異なる反応だ。タコは，自然の生息地から離されると，いたずらをする可能性があり，注意しなければならない。水槽に入れておいたとしたら，その水槽の蓋を押しあげ，脱げ出し，散歩に出かけるかもしれない。科学者は，時々タコに突然訪問を受けることがある。ナポリ動物園の論文，それは，1959 年に書かれたのだが，3 匹のタコにレバーを下げて餌を得る方法を教えようとしたと書かれている。そのうちの 2 匹，アルバートとバートラムは実験に協力したが，チャールズは，賢い頭足動物であったので，実験に協力することを拒否した。チャールズは，科学者たちに水を放ち，実験を終わらせてしまった。装置を壊して。タコの自然な行動や交わりを見ることに興味があれば，海に入ってタコを自分の近くに来させた方が，効果的かもしれない。タコは触手を上げて，あなたを手招きすることさえあるかもしれない。2007 年頃，ピーター・ゴッドフリー＝スミスは，哲学の教授で，ハーバード大学で教えていたのだが，オーストラリアのシドニーに休暇で帰っていた。海中を探検していると，彼は巨大な頭足類に遭遇した。ゴドフリー＝スミスは，自分が目撃した行動に非常に感銘を受け，新たな哲学理論を構築し始めた。自分がした観察に基づいて。人間が頭足類から何を学べるかを発見しようと決意し，ゴッドフリー＝スミスは，頭足類に，どこに導いてくれるか任せてみた。ある海洋旅行中に，別の頭足類がゴッドフリー＝スミスの同僚の手を引いて，タコの生息地を 10 分間ツアーした。「それは，まるで，私の同僚が，8 本足の小さな子供に導かれて，海底を渡っているかのようだった！」泳げない人の場合には，どうやって海の生き物を自分の方に引き寄せることができるだろうか？ カーン家の人々は，「コーラルワールド」で，それは，イスラエルのエイラートにあるのだが，この問題を解決した。その建物の最下層は実際に紅海に建設され，「人間展示場」を作り出している。多くの水族館で行われる海洋生物のパフォーマンスではなく，人が，「人間水槽」にいるのである。そこでは，好奇心旺盛な魚や海洋生物が，海の中を自由に泳ぎながら，あなたを見にやってくるのだ。良い印象を与えるために，素敵な服を着たいと思う人がいるかもしれない。

MET 2023 追 (4) 解答

解答付き英文を見ながら，英語の音声をもう一度聞いてみよう。

The friendly person, who had fed (**and**)[1] socialized with them, got a completely different reaction (**from**)[2] the cephalopods than the other person (**who**)[3] had not. When taken (**from**)[4] their natural habitat, octopuses can be mischievous, so (**watch**)[5] out. They can push (**the**)[6] lids off their tanks, escape, (**and**)[7] go for a walk. Scientists sometimes (**get**)[8] surprise visits. A paper from the Naples Zoological Station, written (**in**)[9] 1959, talks about trying to teach three octopuses (**to**)[10] pull a lever down (**for**)[11] food. Two of them, Albert and Bertram, cooperated (**with**)[12] the experiment, but Charles, a clever cephalopod, refused to (**do**)[13] so. He shot water (**at**)[14] the scientists and ended the experiment (**by**)[15] breaking the equipment. If you are interested (**in**)[16] seeing their natural behavior and interactions, getting into the (**sea**)[17] and having them come to (**you**)[18] might work better. They may (**even**)[19] raise a tentacle to motion you (**over**)[20]. Around 2007, Peter Godfrey-Smith, a philosophy professor teaching at Harvard University, was home (**on**)[21] vacation in Sydney, Australia. Exploring in the ocean, (**he**)[22] came across a giant cephalopod. Godfrey-Smith was (**so**)[23] impressed by the behavior he witnessed that (**he**)[24] started developing philosophy theories based on his observations. Determined to (**find**)[25] out what humans could learn (**from**)[26] cephalopods, Godfrey-Smith let them guide him. (**On**)[27] one ocean trip, another cephalopod took Godfrey-Smith's colleague by (**the**)[28] hand on a 10-minute tour (**of**)[29] the octopus's home, "as if (**he**)[30] were being led across the (**sea**)[31] floor by a very (**small**)[32], eightlegged child!" How can you get (**sea**)[33] creatures to come to you (**if**)[34] you don't swim? The Kahn family has solved (**this**)[35] with "Coral World" in Eilat, Israel. The lowest floor (**of**)[36] the building is actually constructed in the Red Sea, creating (**a**)[37] "human display." Rather than the sea-life performances at many aquariums, (**you**)[38] find yourself in a "people tank," where curious (**fish**)[39] and sea creatures, swimming freely in the (**ocean**)[40], come to look at (**you**)[41]. To make a good impression, (**you**)[42] may want to wear (**nice**)[43] clothes.

MET 2023 追 (5)

英語の音声を聞きながら，（　　）の中に，英単語を入れてください。

As you are reading this, (　　　　)¹ probably have a pencil in your (　　　　)². In the center of every pencil (　　　　)³ something called "lead." This dark gray material is (　　　　)⁴ actually lead (Pb), but a different substance, graphite. Graphite has (　　　　)⁵ a major area of research (　　　　)⁶ many years. It is (　　　　)⁷ up of thin layers of carbon (　　　　)⁸ can be easily separated. Indeed, it is (　　　　)⁹ ease of separation that enables the pencil (　　　　)¹⁰ write. As the pencil rubs against (　　　　)¹¹ paper, thin layers of carbon are pulled (　　　　)¹² the pencil lead and left (　　　　)¹³ the paper as lines (　　　　)¹⁴ writing. In 2004, two scientists, Andre Geim and Konstantin Novoselov, were investigating graphite at the University (　　　　)¹⁵ Manchester, in the UK. They were trying (　　　　)¹⁶ see if they could obtain (　　　　)¹⁷ very thin slice of graphite (　　　　)¹⁸ study. Their goal was (　　　　)¹⁹ get a slice of carbon (　　　　)²⁰ was between 10 and 100 layers thick. Even though (　　　　)²¹ university laboratory had the latest scientific equipment, they made (　　　　)²² incredible breakthrough—for what was later (　　　　)²³ become a Nobel Prize-winning discovery—with only a (　　　　)²⁴ roll of sticky tape. In (　　　　)²⁵ BBC News interview, Professor Geim described their technique. He said that (　　　　)²⁶ first step was to put sticky (　　　　)²⁷ on a piece of graphite. (　　　　)²⁸, when the tape is pulled (　　　　)²⁹, a flake of graphite will (　　　　)³⁰ off on the tape. (　　　　)³¹, fold the tape in (　　　　)³², sticking the flake onto the (　　　　)³³ side of the tape. (　　　　)³⁴ pull the tape apart

(   )[35] split the flake. You (   )[36] have two flakes, roughly half as thick (   )[37] before. Fold the tape together once (   )[38] in a slightly different position to avoid having (   )[39] flakes touch each other. Pull (   )[40] apart again, and you (   )[41] now have four thinner flakes than before. Repeat this procedure 10 (   )[42] 20 times, and you're left with (   )[43] very thin flakes attached to your (   )[44]. Finally, you dissolve the tape using chemicals (   )[45] everything goes into a solution.

MET 2023 追（5）日本語訳

問題英文の日本語訳を確認しよう。

これを読んでいるあなたは，おそらく手に鉛筆を持っているだろう。すべての鉛筆の中心には「芯」と呼ばれるものがある。この濃い灰色の物質は実際には鉛（Pb）ではなく，別の物質であるグラファイトだ。グラファイトは長年にわたって主要な研究分野だった。カーボンの薄い層で構成されており，簡単に分離できる。まさに，この分離の容易さこそが鉛筆の書き込みを可能にするのだ。鉛筆が紙を擦ると，カーボンの薄い層が鉛筆の芯から剥がれ，線や文字として紙に残る。2004年，アンドレ・ガイムとコンスタンチン・ノボセロフという2人の科学者が英国のマンチェスター大学でグラファイトを研究していた。彼らは，研究用に非常に薄いグラファイトの膜が得られるかどうかを確認しようとしていた。彼らの目標は，10〜100層の厚さの炭素の膜を得ることだった。大学の研究室には最新の科学機器があったにもかかわらず，安価な粘着テープだけを使って，後にノーベル賞を受賞することになる発見にとって，信じられないような突破口を開いた。BBCニュースのインタビューで，ガイム教授は彼らの技術について説明した。彼によると，最初のステップはグラファイトに粘着テープを貼ることだった。次に，テープを剥がすと，テープ上でグラファイトの薄片が剥がれる。次に，テープを半分に折り，テープの反対側に薄片を貼り付ける。次に，テープを引き離して薄片を分割する。これで，以前の約半分の厚さの2つの薄片ができる。薄片が互いに接触しないように，少し異なる位置でテープをもう一度折る。もう一度引き離すと，前よりも薄い板が4枚になる。この手順を10〜20回繰り返すと，テープに非常に薄い板が多数付着した状態になる。最後に，化学物質を使用してテープを溶解し，すべてが溶液に入ることになる。

MET 2023 追（5）解答

解答付き英文を見ながら，英語の音声をもう一度聞いてみよう。

As you are reading this, (**you**)[1] probably have a pencil in your (**hand**)[2]. In the center of every pencil (**is**)[3] something called "lead." This dark gray material is (**not**)[4] actually lead (Pb), but a different substance, graphite. Graphite has (**been**)[5] a major area of research (**for**)[6] many years. It is (**made**)[7] up of thin layers of carbon (**that**)[8] can be easily separated. Indeed, it is (**this**)[9] ease of separation that enables the pencil (**to**)[10] write. As the pencil rubs against (**the**)[11] paper, thin layers of carbon are pulled (**off**)[12] the pencil lead and left (**on**)[13] the paper as lines (**or**)[14] writing. In 2004, two scientists, Andre Geim and Konstantin Novoselov, were investigating graphite at the University (**of**)[15] Manchester, in the UK. They were trying (**to**)[16] see if they could obtain (**a**)[17] very thin slice of graphite (**to**)[18] study. Their goal was (**to**)[19] get a slice of carbon (**which**)[20] was between 10 and 100 layers thick. Even though (**their**)[21] university laboratory had the latest scientific equipment, they made (**their**)[22] incredible breakthrough—for what was later (**to**)[23] become a Nobel Prize-winning discovery—with only a (**cheap**)[24] roll of sticky tape. In (**a**)[25] BBC News interview, Professor Geim described their technique. He said that (**the**)[26] first step was to put sticky (**tape**)[27] on a piece of graphite. (**Then**)[28], when the tape is pulled (**off**)[29], a flake of graphite will (**come**)[30] off on the tape. (**Next**)[31], fold the tape in (**half**)[32], sticking the flake onto the (**other**)[33] side of the tape. (**Then**)[34] pull the tape apart (**to**)[35] split the flake. You (**now**)[36] have two flakes, roughly half as thick (**as**)[37] before. Fold the tape together once (**more**)[38] in a slightly different position to avoid having (**the**)[39] flakes touch each other. Pull (**it**)[40] apart again, and you (**will**)[41] now have four thinner flakes than before. Repeat this procedure 10 (**or**)[42] 20 times, and you're left with (**many**)[43] very thin flakes attached to your (**tape**)[44]. Finally, you dissolve the tape using chemicals (**so**)[45] everything goes into a solution.

MET 2023 追（6）

英語の音声を聞きながら，（　　　）の中に，英単語を入れてください。

Geim and Novoselov then looked at the solution, (　　　　)[1] were surprised to see that (　　　)[2] thin flakes were flat and (　　　　)[3] rolled up
—and even more surprised (　　　　)[4] the flakes were as thin (　　　　)[5]
only 10 layers of graphite. As graphite conducts electricity, it (　　　　)[6]
only a matter of weeks before (　　　　)[7] were studying whether these thin
sheets could (　　　　)[8] used in computer chips. By 2005, (　　　　)[9]
had succeeded in separating a single layer (　　　　)[10] graphite. As this
does not (　　　　)[11] naturally, this new material was given (　　　　)[12]
new name: graphene. Graphene is only one (　　　　)[13] thick, and perhaps
the thinnest material in (　　　　)[14] universe. It is one of the (　　　　)[15]
two-dimensional (2D) materials known, and forms a six-sided, honeycomb-patterned structure. (　　　　)[16] addition, it is possibly the lightest
and strongest substance (　　　　)[17] on earth. It is (　　　　)[18] excellent
at carrying electricity. In fact, at laboratory temperatures (20–25°C),
graphene conducts electricity faster (　　　　)[19] any known substance.
This has (　　　　)[20] to manufacturers investing in further research because
graphene-based batteries could last three (　　　　)[21] longer and be
charged five times faster than lithium-ion batteries. Graphene (　　　　)[22]
been called a super-material because of its amazing properties. (　　　　)[23]
is 1,000 times lighter than paper (　　　　)[24] close to being totally transparent. It allows 98% (　　　　)[25] light to pass through it (　　　　)[26] at
the same time (　　　　)[27] is so dense that (　　　　)[28] one molecule of
helium gas cannot pass through it. (　　　　)[29] can also convert light into

electricity.   (   )³⁰ is 200 times stronger than steel (   )³¹ weight: So strong in fact, that (   )³² you could make a 1 m^2 (   )³³ of graphene, it would weigh (   )³⁴ than a human hair (   )³⁵ be strong enough to hold the weight (   )³⁶ a cat. Quite simply, this material (   )³⁷ in pencil lead has the potential (   )³⁸ revolutionize the development of computer chips, rechargeable batteries, and strong, light-weight materials.

MET 2023 追（6）日本語訳

問題英文の日本語訳を確認しよう。

次に，ガイムとノボセロフは溶液を観察し，その薄片が平らで丸まっていないことを見て驚いた。そして，その薄片がわずか10層のグラファイトと同じくらい薄かったことにさらに驚いた。グラファイトは電気を通すため，わずか数週間後には，彼らは，これらの薄い膜がコンピューターチップに使用できるかどうか研究し始めていた。2005年までに，彼らはグラファイトの単層を分離することに成功した。これは自然界には存在しないため，この新しい素材にはグラフェンという新しい名前が付けられた。グラフェンは原子1個の厚さしかなく，おそらく宇宙で最も薄い材料だ。これは知られている数少ない二次元（2D）材料の1つであり，6面からなるハチの巣模様の構造を形成している。加えて，それはおそらく地球上で知られている中で最も軽くて強い物質だ。送電にも優れている。もっと言うと，実験室温度（20 〜 25℃）では，グラフェンは知られているどの物質よりも速く電気を伝導する。グラフェンを使った電池はリチウムイオン電池に比べて3倍長持ちし，5倍速く充電できるため，メーカーはさらなる研究に投資するようになった。グラフェンはその驚くべき特性からスーパーマテリアルと呼ばれている。紙の1,000倍の軽さで，ほぼ透明に近い素材だ。光の98%を通過させるが，同時にヘリウムガスの1分子さえも通過できないほど密度が高いのだ。光を電気に変換することもできる。同じ重さなら鋼鉄の200倍の強度がある。実際，非常に強いため，グラフェン膜が1平方メートル作成できた場合，その重さは人間の髪の毛よりも軽く，猫の体重に耐えるのに十分な強度がある。簡単に言えば，鉛筆の芯に含まれるこの素材は，コンピューター チップ，充電式バッテリー，強力で軽量な素材の開発に革命を起こす可能性を秘めている。

MET 2023 追（6）解答

解答付き英文を見ながら，英語の音声をもう一度聞いてみよう。

Geim and Novoselov then looked at the solution, (**and**)[1] were surprised to see that (**the**)[2] thin flakes were flat and (**not**)[3] rolled up—and even more surprised (**that**)[4] the flakes were as thin (**as**)[5] only 10 layers of graphite. As graphite conducts electricity, it (**was**)[6] only a matter of weeks before (**they**)[7] were studying whether these thin sheets could (**be**)[8] used in computer chips. By 2005, (**they**)[9] had succeeded in separating a single layer (**of**)[10] graphite. As this does not (**exist**)[11] naturally, this new material was given (**a**)[12] new name: graphene. Graphene is only one (**atom**)[13] thick, and perhaps the thinnest material in (**the**)[14] universe. It is one of the (**few**)[15] two-dimensional (2D) materials known, and forms a six-sided, honeycomb-patterned structure. (**In**)[16] addition, it is possibly the lightest and strongest substance (**known**)[17] on earth. It is (**also**)[18] excellent at carrying electricity. In fact, at laboratory temperatures (20–25℃), graphene conducts electricity faster (**than**)[19] any known substance. This has (**led**)[20] to manufacturers investing in further research because graphene-based batteries could last three (**times**)[21] longer and be charged five times faster than lithium-ion batteries. Graphene (**has**)[22] been called a super-material because of its amazing properties. (**It**)[23] is 1,000 times lighter than paper (**and**)[24] close to being totally transparent. It allows 98% (**of**)[25] light to pass through it (**while**)[26] at the same time (**it**)[27] is so dense that (**even**)[28] one molecule of helium gas cannot pass through it. (**It**)[29] can also convert light into electricity. (**It**)[30] is 200 times stronger than steel (**by**)[31] weight: So strong in fact, that (**if**)[32] you could make a 1 m^2 (**sheet**)[33] of graphene, it would weigh (**less**)[34] than a human hair (**and**)[35] be strong enough to hold the weight (**of**)[36] a cat. Quite simply, this material (**found**)[37] in pencil lead has the potential (**to**)[38] revolutionize the development of computer chips, rechargeable batteries, and strong, light-weight materials.

牧　秀樹（まき　ひでき）

　岐阜大学地域科学部シニア教授。1995 年にコネチカット大学にて博士号（言語学）を取得。研究対象は，言語学と英語教育。
　主な著書：*Essays on Irish Syntax*（共著，2011 年），*Essays on Mongolian Syntax*（共著，2015 年），*Essays on Irish Syntax II*（共著，2017 年），『The Minimal English Test（最小英語テスト）研究』（2018 年），『誰でも言語学』，『最小英語テスト（MET）ドリル』〈標準レベル：高校生から社会人〉，〈センター試験レベル〉，『中学生版 最小英語テスト（jMET）ドリル』（以上，2019 年），「英語 monogrammar シリーズ」『関係詞』『比較』『準動詞』『助動詞・仮定法』『時制・相』『動詞』（監修，以上，2020-2021 年），『金言版 最小英語テスト（kMET）ドリル』（2020 年），『これでも言語学—中国の中の「日本語」』，*Essays on Case*（以上，2021 年），『それでも言語学—ヒトの言葉の意外な約束』，『最小日本語テスト（MJT）ドリル』，『最小中国語テスト（MCT）ドリル』，『最小韓国語テスト（MKT）ドリル』（以上，2022 年），『MCT 中国語実践会話—学びなおしとステップアップ 上海出張・日本紹介』（共著，2023 年），『象の鼻から言語学—主語・目的語カメレオン説』（2023 年），『みんなの言語学入門—日本語と英語の仕組みから未知の言語へ』，『火星人とはなしたよ—地球人のことばは，ほとんどおなじなんだって』（2023 年）［以上，開拓社］，『10 分でわかる！ことばの仕組み』（2023 年，Kindle Direct Publishing），『最小英語テスト（MET）ドリル〈大学入学共通テスト聴解版〉』（2024 年，開拓社）など。

何　海希（か　かいき）

　岐阜大学大学院地域科学研究科在学中。牧秀樹研究室に所属。研究対象は、最小日本語テスト。

最小英語テスト（MET）ドリル
〈大学入学共通テスト読解版〉

ISBN978-4-7589-2339-2　C0082

著作者	牧　秀樹・何　海希	
発行者	武村哲司	
印刷所	日之出印刷株式会社	

2024 年 6 月 12 日　第 1 版第 1 刷発行©

発行所　　株式会社　開拓社

〒112-0013　東京都文京区音羽 1-22-16
電話　（03）5395-7101（代表）
振替　00160-8-39587
https://www.kaitakusha.co.jp